THE GLAM ROCK FILES by Dia

Over the years, every time I start my storytelling, usually whilst doing people's hair, or at a bus stop, or whilst selling people some unusual object from far away, various individuals have remarked "You should write a book, with all your stories."

Well, yes, but exactly which stories from which period of time with which kinds of experiences? Travelling and working extensively in Asia? Driving through Scandinavia, Russia and parts of Eastern Europe in the nineties in search of obscure rave parties? Living as part pf a Guru's entourage in India?

Ultimately perhaps the teenage experiences are the ones which stick most deeply in the consciousness, since they form the bridge from childhood to adulthood. So here is a book completely centered around my experiences of the birth of Glam and other types of rock music in the Seventies. I grew up with the music and the style and the musicians and they have influenced me into becoming the free-spirited Hello Kitty Leopardskin Gothic Queen you know nowadays.

The inspirations for this book come from the following:-

Marc Bolan/Tyrannosaurus Rex, Lou Reed, Iggy Pop, enormously from Freddie Mercury and Queen. Mott the Hoople, Roxy Music and Elton John are other influences.

Thanks to the Golden Lion pub in Fulham (now defunct) for putting up with me and employing me through my transition from country bumpkin to city slicker. To Messrs Keith Emerson and Carl Palmer for allowing me free run of their studio and allowing me to play with their organs (sic). To Robert Plant, for finding it extremely amusing and sexy when I yelled at this bloke in a crimson velvet jacket with long, curly blonde hair "Will you *shut* that bloody bar door!" and for pulling a good pint and grinning whilst customers murmured, "Doesn't that bloke look a bit like Robert Plant...?" "Nah, wassup with yer, he's a bloody barman...!"

But most of all my love and thanks goes to David Bowie, alien, iconic, ever-mysterious David, who woke me up, shook me up, shook me cold, amazed me, turned my head around and whispered into my soul from his spirit state to write this book. David, I always have and always will love you.

Here is:-

The Glam Rock Files

Diana Wilde

Koh Phanang Island

Thailand, S.E. Asia

PROLOGUE

When I was eight years old I discovered that what I had suspected was true; there really *was* magic.

It was accidental. I had been given a Judy Annual for Christmas, with all the usual Good Girl Guide stuff in it, and all the necessary pointers towards being a Good Community Citizen of future charity bazaars, combined with a little teenage romance with a nice boy before the boredom of Real Life began.

But there it was, hidden somewhere between tying knots and baking cakes whilst putting on your eyeshadow and blusher correctly, and the adventures of Tess the Girl Guide;

The Guide to the Zodiac.

At first I was really disappointed not to be a Lion, or even a goat or a bull, but some little insect which could sting people to death and lived under rocks in the desert. However, the description was a spookily accurate summing up of my most secret characteristics and I realised.....this is something I can understand! Sorry, but Being Saved By Jesus had never really caught my attention although I felt empathy with the man for being so misunderstood. But here was a system which made sense to my young but very inquisitive mind.

How this metamorphosised into following Glam Rock artists just a little later in life is perhaps a little obscure.

But after the initiation into Astrology, I received The Lion, the Witch and the Wardrobe as a school Christmas present when I put down 'a book' as my request. I spent quite a lot of time after this walking into the 'outdoor coat' wardrobe at the bottom of the stairs, closing the door in different ways, quickly, slowly, halfway, as I tried my best to get into Narnia.

I read books on cats who had 'humans' not the other way around, including the amazing Grimbold's Other World by Nicholas Stuart Gray. I read books on American wolf spirits and witches and all kinds of esoteric stuff. I used to walk around the playground reading at school breaks and desperately wanted to be old enough to visit the Adult Library section, since by the age of twelve I had virtually exhausted all the junior stuff.

And then these musicians appeared, singing about things which I had read about, places which I had visited in my mind. Not the Heavy Rockers; they mostly sung about Lerve, and disappointment, and getting drunk in bars in Rio and killing someone.

But a new type of musician was appearing on the scene just as I was entering my teens, ones who sung of wizards and warlocks, and ones who sung of spiritual paths of which I had no knowledge but a thirst as big as the ocean for the information they could give me.

All the great Glam Rockers were also steeped to the hilt in mystery, magic and alternative spirituality. That was the real key to their ongoing success, far more than the glitter on their faces and their tight satin pants; they introduced us, their questioning young teenage audience, to a world of myth, magic and alternative possibilities spiritual as well as sexual.

So this is the path to which I became drawn, and since in later years I reached India and spent many years studying with a Guru, learned reiki and meditation, homeopathy, hypnotherapy and yoga, I guess that the earlier influences were well and truly in place from this early exposure. These musicians predated the current obsessions with vampires and wizards, and Harry Potter, and Lord of the Rings, by several decades, and yet helped set the stage for a rebirth in magical interest and spiritual practices which has since swept the world.

So this book is all about the seventies rock musicians who shaped my life.

Many of them have left us now, so I give thanks to all my angels, in the body and out.

All the cats, you know who you are.

Marc Bolan

Mickey Finn

Mick Ronson

Lou Reed

Iggy Pop

Andy Warhol

Jacques Brel

Jean Genet

The New York Dolls

The Velvet Underground

Keith Emerson

Carl Palmer

Freddie Mercury

Brian May

Roger Taylor

Robert Plant

John Bonham

Paul Rodgers

Paul Kossoff

Andy Fraser

Marillion

Camel

And my guiding light, King of my Universe, Keeper of my Soul

David Bowie

Love you all

See you at the party!

CHAPTER ONE – A SOLITARY SOUL

I was the eldest of, as the years went on, four children; a brother two and a half years younger, and twin sisters five years my junior.

It appears that I was always fond of my own company. I can never remember feeling lonely as a small child. I seemed to derive a great sense of joy and peace from my own company, probably because I was never *really* alone in life. Some scene was always going on in my head, played out against the backdrop of real life as opposed to interfering with it.

The moment my parents' attention turned away from me my mind took up the thread again and on progressed the story, whatever it was, often with scenes played out in different ways.

It appears I always had some kind of companion, but not necessarily an imaginary figure; sometimes it was a real cat, sometimes a whole host of characters, and sometimes the story itself was enough of a companion for me in life. I often viewed 'real' people and situations as an interruption to these ongoing fantasy serials. Probably I still do...

One time my parents thought I was asleep or playing somewhere. Ultimately they discovered me sitting quietly behind the sofa, in one of my 'other worlds', carefully and systematically peeling the wallpaper off the walls, fascinated especially by the corner bits.

My brother seemed simply to slip into my life at some point; I cannot remember much fanfare at his birth, and only one incident stood out, that of him receiving a toy tool set for his second birthday and knocking a great chip out of the then brand new gas cooker with the hammer! Personally he did not disturb me too much; I regarded him as somewhat of a curiosity.

The twins, however, were a different matter. At some point when I was around four years old I started becoming aware that my mother was what was called 'pregnant,' and after some more time I was told that she was having twins. Twin girls. I think even then we were told that. I don't know why, but it appeared that thirty five was somewhat of a difficult age to have twins, so they already knew the sex.

From this moment forwards, life changed dramatically.

At my school, for instance, there was a whole lesson, it appeared, devoted to choosing possible names for my twin sisters! Everything now seemed to revolve around this subject, ad nauseum, until it became close to the time and my mother went into hospital.

That in itself was a drama, since it was seven weeks earlier than predicted. I had no idea what that meant, but one day she came back from hospital. Without the twins.

I was puzzled and even looked in her bag to see where they were. However, it turned out that *they* were still at the hospital, in something called an incubator.

I had no clue what this was all about, but a lot of coming and going and animated talking was going on, something about 'seven weeks premature' and some weight stories, some three pounds plus ounces, for one, some four pounds plus ounces for another.

I still had no clue what it meant. With hindsight, probably my mother had a very difficult time. But it was 1961 and in those days young children were told fairy stories about both birth and death.

My mother eventually brought home these two tiny, ugly (as babies are in truth) pink hamsters and settled down to looking after them. She was swollen, bloated, preoccupied every moment of night and day, no more stories or double sided jigsaws now! I have never wanted children all of my life...not exclusively but especially from that moment,

After about four or five months, though, came the *real* big change, one from which I have never recovered. I was a girl, they were girls, and the house had two large bedrooms and one boxroom. Therefore sometime during the winter of 1961/2, I found myself extricated from my cosy little bedroom and plonked into a single bed in one of the large rooms. A double bed was installed in it as well, and now I was to share a room with The Twins.

Never in my life since then have I been able to share a room with *anyone* unless it was the only option (ie paying fifteen pounds for a hostel dorm as opposed to eighty for a private). I cannot stand to this day to sleep in the same *room* as another human being, let alone the same bed!

Only in my wildest days did I spend the complete nights with men. But that's another story...

Parents never appear to think about the effect their decisions will have on their children. I have no idea why. Had my sisters been new brothers, maybe I would have had a very different life.

But the Universe has its ways...

I was, as the eldest but as well as being the eldest, kind of the Golden Girl of my family, quite literally for a start with my head of shiny golden-silver hair.

But this also spilled over into my actual life. Sets of encyclopaedia were bought, and at six years old I was sent for private piano lessons.

At school I did well, but it was never, *ever,* considered, planned or allowed for that I would fail in *anything!* It was alright for me not to be especially sporty since if my fingers got broken playing with hard balls it would affect my father's ambitions for me as a pianist. And it was alright not to be too interested in science subjects since that was not the path he had in mind for me. But at the subjects he decided in advance that I should be 'good at', I was expected to get top marks.

It appeared that my parents had these great hopes for me. Post-war parents often did, I suppose. But again, your hopes and dreams for another human being, are not necessarily those which that person might wish for themselves, and if it comes to a clash of wills...

Ah, the amount of disappointing children and disappointed parents there must be on anti-depressants these days, and even in mental institutions, just for these reasons...

But that's another story...and not mine. I chose another way out.

Magic. The creation of fantasy worlds as a substitute now for what I saw as a second-rate kind of a life. The endless retreats into Narnia, and later Middle Earth, all bound up with the great deep well of knowledge which contained astrology, palmistry, numerology and all kinds of other pagan magic.

A fascination with anything and everything esoteric permeated every aspect of my life, and my youngest methods of slipping off into parallel 'other worlds' were now reinforced by more and more learning. My thirst for knowledge was unquenchable and I rapidly devoured library books at a rate no-one else could match; by twelve years old, I already yearned to be allowed to enter the Adult Library.

Despite my constant pleas to convert the attic of the house my parents bought when I was eleven, still 'a room of one's own' was but a distant memory, and a future hope. Right now I was stuck in the same kind of situation in the new house, which did have an attic, but not, unfortunately, one with a little ventilated, windowed box room in it for a secretive little squirrel.

If they had bought a four-bedroom, again my life might have turned out differently.

But better? Well...wait and see!

I am just setting the scene here, as it puzzles even me sometimes how it all came about, how the Glam Rock men became my personal heroes and the gateway to the freedom I so desperately craved! I do not know what the constraints and deepest yearnings of childhood have brought forth in me, as even to this day I see nothing as impossible.

And all because of the years I am about to write about, the all-important, transformative years between the age of twelve and eighteen, in my case taking place between 1968 and 1975...

The Glam Rock years.

CHAPTER TWO - KIM

After the transition from Junior School to Grammar school I found myself in Form Eleven, House of Rome. Form Ten was the first level of the nine allocated, so I was in the second level; these were the top two streams. It was never, ever, a consideration on my parents' part that I would be *lower* than the top two streams.

In the second year of Grammar school, Form Twenty, I met Kim Pimperton. Both she and I had been switched from other forms where we knew people; now, marooned in a sea of strangers, we were seated next to each other in class.

She looked like Yoko Ono. Not 'a bit like', but almost identical. Of Welsh ancestry, she and all her family except for her mother bore the thick, dark hair and sallow, almost olive skin of their race. Kim's hair was long and parted in the middle; its thickness made it stick out slightly as Yoko's did. I had long, floppy hair which left my head a dark gold colour but after an inch or so turned always to a natural platinum blonde. I did not wear glasses, but the images stuck with people anyway; they called us 'John and Yoko.'

I genuinely cannot remember much of my life other than the yearnings and the magical bits before I turned twelve; somehow, after that, everything changed and it was in the summers of 1969 and 1970 that the seeds of what kind of a person I was to become in life were really sown.

It began with the summer holidays of 1969 and the advent of Music. Music had certainly been *there* all of my life. Aged six, the eldest child of a man whose musical possibilities had been cut short by the loss of three and a half fingers in a mining accident at the age of seventeen, I was 'given the opportunity' to take piano lessons from a private teacher.

In reality it was never an 'option'. It was my father's wish; I did not refuse. I was just six. Even aged eight your own tastes are beginning to form (reiki teachings here) and I might have said no, but at six I was still really just a small child.

Every Friday I would learn from Mr Bentley, and every other day of the week, I would practice for half an hour piano and half an hour theory. This is as well as school, and it is a large chunk out of a child's day.

One time I decided to drop it. My father sulked for a week, and was overjoyed when I resumed. This set the tone for the future, in many ways...

But six years on now in the summer of '69, I am referring not to music, but Music!!

My dad had a penchant for bringing home unheard-of singles by unknown artists, which he was sure would be a hit, and he was often right, as with Yellow River by Tony Christie, In the Summertime by Mungo Jerry, and Spirit in the Sky by Norman Greenbaum.

I particularly liked the last one, and so did many a teen; it began to be played everywhere, and there was a kind of a psychedelic video accompanying it on Top of the Pops. The dance you did to it had you swaying with your hands in the air.

There was talk of 'hippies' surrounding this single. I began to try and find out what they were as I rather liked this kind of swaying, entrancing music.

At twelve years old therefore I was listening to pop songs here, there, everywhere. The Beatles had split up now, and as Kim and I drifted towards teenhood, we began to notice the four different styles emerging from this former Supergroup.

The most obviously powerful were from John Lennon with the political songs Bangladesh and Power to the People. But even more powerful in a far more subtle form was the hit by George Harrision, 'My Sweet Lord,' which we sang along to. Kim had the single; I did not; my dad bought only singles which *he* liked, even if we *did* like some of them...

So it was at Kim's house that I first heard the B-side...Govindam.

We sang along dutifully, therefore, to this too, 'John and Yoko,' now rapidly developing a taste for floppy blouses, jeans, cords, 'Jesus sandals ' long strings of beads and Afghan coats, which we had discovered were things that 'hippies' wore. Two twelve and something year olds singing quite clearly and with no trouble in pronunciation, 'Hare Krishna, Hare Krishna, Hare Rama, Hare Rama,' and 'Govindam, Adi Purusham...'

Considering that now, as I write, I have spent the last twenty three years living mostly in India, Nepal and south east Asia, the initiated disciple of a high Indian guru and a regular mantra practitioner, I wonder...how our lives are shaped by the smallest of twists and turns...

But that all came much later...

Autumn of 1969 came around, I turned thirteen, and Kim and I became more 'weird' in the eyes of our new term class, Form Thirty. We had spent the summer, and now spent any available free time, wandering around dressed, for all intents and purposes, as 'John and Yoko'.

Our new class again had some girls I knew in it again from Junior school. They were friendly enough, but they had brought one girl along in their group from the previous two years who, it appeared, absolutely hated me on sight! I have no idea why.

Hindsight again perhaps has the answers, but they were not details that I had thought through at the time; however, Ruth Ellis, this girl, was fattish and dumpy, with specs and a bowl haircut. As well as being unprepossessing, she was highly dominant in the group of my ex-classmates and strived quite successfully to exclude me. She bore, too, this is also with hindsight, the name of the last woman to hang in Britain!

I was being cut from the group of my ex-classmates and at the same time I had my loyal friend here in this other group, so...divisions were highly magnified now. The little group of

Form Thirty Elite 'lived' on one side of what was our 'base' classroom, and 'we' (Kim, myself and a few other girls who seemed to like rock music a lot too) 'lived' on the other side, near the windows!

By the following spring I was buying the music papers along with Kim, following the ever-expanding amount of amazing rock musicians who were mostly in America but were also beginning to emerge in England too. I did not know too much about them, but every time we came across a new, interesting-sounding group, we would try our best to find something from them somewhere on the radio. Kim had some records of her own; I just had my dad's to play.

We spent most of the summer of 1970 bemoaning the fact that we were too young (and penniless) to go to Woodstock and the Isle of Wight festival, especially the latter since it was at least in the same country.

For at the latter were playing Kim's new heroes, a British rock band called Free. They had already had a single out, an exciting, raunchy rock track called 'Alright Now,' and an album. In fact, several albums.

Kim, whose parents indulged her with records as mine, who were wealthier, did not, had a much better collection already than I even though she was actually about eight months younger and technically should have been in the year below me if she had not been 'gifted'. Technically, we should never have met...!

Free had a lovely bluesy rock feel, a great, tight band with a talented bassist, ballsy drummer, wonderfully soulful singer named Paul Rodgers, with whom Kim was deeply in love both musically and image-wise, and one of the greatest rock guitarists ever to grace this earth for a short while, Paul Kossoff. We spent a lot of the summer holidays listening to Kim's albums and becoming deeply melancholy with every new song, in accordance with this type of music's requirements.

Our Bibles were, in ascending order; Sounds, which came out every Wednesday, New Musical Express (NME) which came out on Fridays, and Melody Maker (MM) which came out sometimes on Thursdays, sometimes Fridays.

The latter pair could sometimes be switched around in preference order, since although the MM was the more serious 'heavy rock' paper, NME could also yield up some gems, and had a lighter, more entertaining approach for the butterfly-minded reader who wanted to know more about what the rockers had for breakfast and liked to wear in the bath, less about the chord progression from A major to D minor on the bass solo...

There *was* another thing with the NME, or more truthfully, *would* be another thing in my future...this music paper was also much more open towards what might be called at this stage 'alternative styles of music' as opposed to Hard Rock, Blues and Progressive Rock.

But that is to come...

For now, our weekly perusal of our three Bibles (usually during Maths classes since the poor, unfortunate teacher, who was called Mr Clarke and had dandruff in his hair, beard and eyebrows, could not control us) continued apace through the cold winter.

Knees and calves almost bare in only regulation thin tights, opaque not permitted, we formed small groups on the increasingly freezing cold days on the school playing fields at break times. It was here that the real learning took place, as we swapped sandwiches for fruit or cakes and practiced levitation (sorry, no idea where we got this from).

We learned about sex by group readings of bits of The Naked Ape by Desmond Morris, which was currently being serialised in one of the newspapers and was sneaked by someone - Elaine, I think, an only child who was told the Facts of Life a bit earlier than most of us - from her parents.

Most important of all for Kim and I, it was here that we devoured endless information about our dawning pop and rock heroes...

I have no idea where I got my other musical influences from. I did listen to the radio a *lot.*

I tended to get up early, especially in the summer, and do a lot of things before school. Have a shower first, then make the tea for my parents and the coffee I was already fond of for myself.

Then, making some cornflakes with milk but no sugar (already I was on the Teenage Diet trip) I would sit and quickly skim through whatever I was supposed to learn for school, and do the homework if any, all this whilst drinking my coffee and listening to the radio, since I had piano practice at seven forty five until eight thirty every day except Mondays, which were my current lesson days.

Tony Blackburn *did* irritate me, but he played a lot of good songs by both pop artists and those a little more obscure and unusual.

One time he told this story about a fire engine whose crew went to rescue an old lady's cat stuck up a tree but ran over it when they were leaving, and he was giggling so much that loads of people rang in to complain. It was dark humour very much in tune with my own, so I forgave him for being a bit of a nerd.

There were one or two times that summer/autumn that he announced the deaths of a couple of musicians. Jimi Hendrix was one, Janis Joplin another. I did not really know who they were except that they had played at Woodstock, and now they were dead, people were acknowledging them as geniuses, legends in their own time taken too soon.

It felt strange listening to this usually glib, rather silly radio presenter talking about anything serious and important to him, so I began to listen out for more of their music.

There was another radio programme I listened to from the age of about thirteen. It was called Sounds of the Seventies. I often fell asleep listening to it, as it was on late in the night. But slowly...I was hearing a huge range of interesting music not played anywhere else.

Somehow I had acquired this little radio, made of orange plastic, with a single mono headphone, and I began to listen to it a lot. It was small so I could take it anywhere, into the woods and fields, up the trees I loved to climb and sit, pretending to be a cat.

I was right on the border of childhood and teenhood, still engaged in these tomboy pursuits, but listening now to this Music which was beginning to dominate my life. Slowly, slowly, I was developing my own tastes too. Not my father's tastes, and not even Kim's, but mine. My own.

CHAPTER THREE - FREE AT LAST

Kim had always told me that her dream was to see Free live onstage.

The very thought of being able to do this was intoxicating; listening to a record was one thing; to actually go and see the same musicians live, playing this wonderful music right in our faces, was altogether a different matter. Almost like we really *were* young hippies, able to go and watch the same bands who had played at the Isle of Wight festival, which was already achieving cult status and became a legend in its own time.

By now, since we had returned to school, you could not prise Kim and I apart with a screwdriver, and my 'lucky' chum had sometimes accompanied my family on weekends in my father's bizarre and gigantic black Ford Zephyr with its eye-catching (?!) nude lady figurehead on the bonnet.

We had one problem in this Brave New World of our friendship and our growing addiction to rock bands...money.

Kim had an idea, knowledge, in fact, of how we fledgling teenagers could become parentally independent on the financial front and achieve Our Dream.

Potato picking. We call it 'Spud Bashing' up north, and it would occur conveniently in the school holidays in October.

This lucrative activity, available to us for the whole week of the October break, involved my a) staying over at Kim's house, b) us all being picked up next morning at five thirty am in an open truck from the end of her road and c) spending an entire day picking up potatoes churned up by a digger-thingy and putting them into baskets, for which we were paid per basket. The average to be earned per day from this was a whopping one pound thirty pence. Five times this was to us an absolute fortune!

From this wonderfully liberating activity (truly, for me!) I made enough money to do something I had never done before; buy a completely new fashionable 'tank top' as opposed to something my aunt or grandma tried to copy by hand. It came in what would nowadays be Rasta coloured stripes, in a stretchy wool, and came with the proviso that MY MUM WAS NOT ALLOWED EVER TO WASH OR IRON IT, since she believed that 'crinkle skirts' for instance looked a mess and viewed them as a challenge for her iron.

I was by now already exploring the boundaries of what a parentally-dependent girl of thirteen can make with the available jumble-sale clothes and jewellery and scraps of fabric I could scrounge or otherwise accumulate from aunts and grandparents.

Two more items completed the break forever with the Parents As Role Models; firstly the purchase of my own first single ever, the Rolling Stones' 'Brown Sugar'.

Secondly, since the record shop in Sheffield and the ticket office were one and the same, the revered Wilson Peck on the corner near the City Hall.....the purchase, jointly by Kim and I, of two tickets to see Free in late February of 1971.

The cold of the winter passed slowly, I turned fourteen.

Christmas came, and we went, Kim and I along with the rest of our classes, to the School Disco, wearing miniskirts. Kim impressed me with the way she pulled a sort of 'cool' face and swished her long hair when she danced. I danced too, but really the music, mostly Tamla Motown with its songs of spurned or deserted lovers, did not move me in any way.

Some girls, for instance, were almost in tears as they danced to 'Now that you've gone, all that's left is a band of gold...' and 'Tears of a Clown' and suchlike. But since marriage, children and Lerve, at least this kind, were not my interests, I waited for My Sweet Lord, Power to the People and Spirit in the Sky to move my body. We were even lucky enough to get Alright Now!

The year turned, the days grew fractionally lighter.

On February twenty sixth, 1971 for the first time ever Kim and I took the bus into Sheffield and walked slowly up the long incline to the hallowed temple of Sheffield City Hall.

I can still recollect that special 'City Hall smell' which heralded my seeing some of the best rock bands ever to make music in the coming few years, perhaps in my lifetime too. I don't know really what the smell was, some combination of the hall itself and the cleaning fluid used perhaps, but to us it was as heady as incense, and as intoxicating.

So were many of the other people who roamed around confidently in the entry hall with their long hair, Afghan coats, love beads, joss sticks, and of course.....jeans. *Everyone* wore jeans. Preferably old jeans, flared and frayed at the ends.

I had rather a penchant for black, in various fabrics, especially velvet, and jeans were not my favourite thing, but black always has and always will work the Dark Trick, so I was accepted into the fold, since much worse than black were...horror of horrors...New Jeans!

These people at the gig that night were Cool. I could see that immediately. They intimidated slightly, but even small, young newbies were respected simply by the fact that we were all here to see Free.

We took our seats, which were about eight rows from the front, and heard a really interesting support act called Amazing Blondel, who basically played their own versions of Medieval music. They sung an amazing acapella song called Gaudete, and told a one-liner joke which I still remember; 'If Typhoo put the tea in Britain, who put the C*#t in Scunthorpe?'

Then, after a break and much time spent in the toilets trying to pee in advance, it was time for the main band, and Kim's dream came true as Free took the stage.

I was a gobsmacked little blonde fourteen year old, almost bowled over by a huge surge to the front of 'older' (fifteen to twenty five year old mostly) kids, but we took it in our stride and stood up too as a packed hall greeted Free with yells, whoops, raised arms and spilt beer. And then.....the band played on...

A great wall of sound poured out of the amps, guitars wailing, bassline booming, the drums full power and Paul Rodgers' voice soaring confidently over it all. This was not hearing the songs on Kim's or my parents' stereo record player. This...was a completely different experience! The real musicians who played the music were here, right in front of us, in Sheffield, they had faces, names, sweat, feedback, perhaps the odd mistake, although I never heard any...

My first rock concert!

It was a great night from beginning to end as we all sang, hummed or grunted in some cases along to all the songs we had learned in our Summer of Love.

Kim, in her top and Jeans, gazed up in wonder at her hero Paul Rodgers, who cut a dashing figure for sure with his long, dark, wavy, Natural hair, Natural facial stubble/almost-beard and purple Starred T-shirt with flared sleeves, a must-have in our circles after this gig. And of course, Jeans. Very nicely-fitting, flared Jeans. The rest of the band, including the doomed genius Paul Kossoff, were all together, and they were Alright Now.

For the last few songs we joined the other people in the audience in clambering onto our seats, trying to balance, clap along with raised arms and head-bang, all without getting tipped back down by the flip action of the old cinema-style seats. At the end of concerts like this, the halls got used to having to repair the first few blocks of seats afterwards.

I was *really* impressed by some of the headbanging! Some people could swirl their necks around in a complete arc, hair flying. I resolved to practice hard for the next time.

After a second encore and a great wave of applause, the band finally left the stage and the house lights came back on, leaving people slightly confused as they slowly came back to being just ordinary working class folk from Yorkshire and not Cool Cats from Mississippi.

My dad and Uncle Don (who was not my uncle per se but my dad's lifelong drinking friend) had arranged to pick us up. They had thankfully parked some distance away so that we didn't have to look 'uncool' getting picked up by relatives instead of wandering off down the street chatting with other Cool People and popping into the pub to dissect the band's technique as though we were all peer musicians.

I really had enjoyed the evening. It was an eye-opener for sure, and a taste of what Real Life could be like. Kim was over the moon, and already planning our next trip to see Free when they came our way again.

But there was another side to this visit of mine to see Free, namely a bargain that I had struck with Kim, and that was that she would come with me in the month of April to see another band.

This outfit was basically a duo. They were not a rock band. They were something new, a whispered hippie word which was filtering through the grapevine. I had heard of them through the music magazines we obsessed over weekly, and on John Peel's Sounds of the Seventies, which I listened to under the bedclothes every week night between ten pm and midnight on my tiny radio with its mono headphone, often falling asleep in the process.

Their name in full was Tyrannosaurus Rex. They were comprised of just two men, a long-haired bongo/drum player named Mickey Finn (for real!) and a diminutive creature of Jewish origin with the prettiest face you could ever find in this world, topped by a cascade of long, dark curls.

His name, originally Mark Feld, was now Marc Bolan. He played acoustic guitar and sung all his own songs, about wizards and dragons, sacred journeys and castles. He wrote poetry and spoke of Tolkien's Lord of the Rings, which at that time only I seemed to have heard of amongst my peers.

He himself was an elf sent to earth, the most beautiful thing I had ever seen.

And Kim and I had tickets to see him and his little band, in two months' time on the seventeenth of April 1971.

CHAPTER FOUR - T.REXTASY PART ONE– 'I TOUCHED HIS ARM!'

At my school among the 'school elite,' the Creme de la Creme, little girls! it was cool to like rock bands, and even more so, Progressive rock bands, preferably Heavy Intellectual ones, especially if they sung Relevant Songs with Earnest Lyrics. And had beards, and of course wore Jeans.

T.Rex were a different proposition. They had a strange reputation, their worth as yet not proven on the Earnest songs front, and their heaviness in serious doubt with their acoustic guitars and bongos, and Marc's sultry, warbling little voice.

Since he had already published a book of poetry entitled The Warlock of Love, and he did burn incense and mention Wizards, he was sufficiently Cool enough that although the Jeans brigade approached him warily, they did give him the benefit of the doubt in these days. The future would change all that.....

Marc's image, however, was a different thing. Although he had long hair, and sometimes wore Jeans, his general garb was a lot closer to my at-present secret, soon-to-be-outed fascination with all things shiny, satiny, velvety, sparkly, sequinned and animal print.

And his hair changed my life forever!

His lush curls cascaded over his shoulders and framed that impossibly pretty face with its lovely eyes and cupids-bow lips. His were natural, dark, almost black. Mine were.....not....

What a job of work it was to transform my naturally light blonde, straight hair into a negative halo to compliment his positive one. This is how.....

First I would wash it. Then I sectioned it and plaited each section to the end. Then I would turn up the end of each one twice and wrap it around the plait, securing each piece with elastic bands. Then...

I have sometimes wondered how come I ended up being a self-taught maker of dreadlocks and other unusual hair extensions and the like, with no hairdresser training. I guess I have just explained this to myself.

Well, then, I would sit under my mother's cover-type hairdryer and bake the said sections for at least an hour until a) they were crisp and b) I had a burned scalp. Leave to cool for some time, remove all elastic bands and plaits, shake out and hey presto! A white-blonde Marc Bolan Afro to be proud of! At this time I was not aware of The Perm and the hours it would have saved me.

April seventeenth dawned, and set, and it was the evening and time to go again to Sheffield City Hall with Kim. The streets were lighter tonight as we walked up from the bus station. My friend seemed less comfortable with this concert than I had been with hers, but she took it in her stride.

This time we were old hands. By now I also had an Afghan Coat, and my silky print top, velvet pants and waist-length beads were much less out of place here than at the previous gig. And my hair made me visible from a distance of at least half a mile!

Our seats were only a little way back. When T.Rex, as they called themselves for short, came onstage the reaction was not like it had been for Free. It was no less positive, but the kind of audience they attracted were very cool and peaceful and sat in their seats nicely, only standing up towards the end of the show.

No seat-ripping this time. Some people did stand up, including us, but swayed on the spot or danced to the soaring, spiralling sounds of vocals, acoustic guitar and bongos with their arms raised in the air, gazing into space.

It was a strangely tranquil atmosphere. Surprisingly there were very few people of our age, most were seventeen and over. There were just a few little teenies, younger than us even, but although they were a little excited there was no screaming, just big eyes and soft, awed faces.

Marc Bolan was absolutely enthralling. His speaking voice between songs was as soft and cultured as his singing one, sultry, sexy and hypnotic. He sat on the floor cross-legged for most of the set, another thing to love about him, whilst Mickey Finn, also very good-looking with long, straight black hair swishing around, and a cool attitude, stood behind beating his bongos and other various types of percussion.

I was totally in love with this beautiful creature by the end of the concert. Rock bands were cool, but this was something different. Even as an inexperienced concert-goer I could tell that this was.....a rising star. A legend in the making.

I was right. And how!

By midsummer most of my peer group at school's cautious reaction to Tyrannosaurus Rex had turned to outright avoidance and condemnation. If you liked T.Rex you were a traitor to the Cause of Earnestness. And Jeans.

The single Ride a White Swan, which had preceded their spring tour, had contained Wiccan references, and therefore was still acceptable.

But the next single, a fully electric offering called Hot Love, was riding the charts with its singalong chorus even as we were mounting the City Hall steps. This in turn paved the way for a new song in July entitled 'Get it On', which blasted into people's living rooms on Top of the Pops to the shock of many a parent as their little girls (and maybe boys) were transfixed by this pretty creature with his corkscrew curls, elfin face, satin pants, sequined jacket and glitter sprinkled over his cheeks!

My dad was not impressed and walked out to do the garden, muttering something about fairies, leaving me to smirk, thinking 'He knows nothing; Marc is a Warlock!'

I first heard the phrase 'Glam Rock' not in the celebrated pages of Sounds, New Musical Express or Melody Maker, or on any of the night programmes, but in the school toilets.

I had gone in there, but the other two girls in there from my class must have thought I had left again because they began talking about me. "Ooo does she think she is?" asked one (a common Northern phrase used to speak about anyone who dares to be different. I think they were referring to my 'corkscrew curls'...)

"Ah dunt know," came the reply over the sound of the hand-dryer. "She's into that Glam Rock, yer know," the second speaker continued.

So that is how I discovered the name for my new fixation.

Back to Get It On. I didn't care a hoot for this label of Glam Rock, was rather proud in fact, for T.Rex's latest single was everything I had ever wanted to hear from Marc Bolan and about a hundred times more, as he swaggered loveably around the stage on TOTP, thrusting out his little hips and tossing his curls.

He murmured things, and made small, throaty noises into the the mic in a way which made me squirm on the edge of my chair, which was normally my father's seat, but was unofficially designated to me for the weekly TOTP experience. At one point, to the united ecstasy of every teenage female, and many teenage males, in the country, he whispers 'take me!'

If it were nowadays, of course, I would have replayed this eight hundred times a day on my iphone. But it was 1971 and once a week on TOTP if you were lucky, had to suffice, not even a video recorder or a rewind facility! Just that moment to capture and live on for days!

I kind of knew without knowing what he meant by 'take me'; even then, as I approached fifteen, I knew that usually men 'took' women (courtesy of some 'bodice rippers' I had found in the library) so it was a little puzzling dynamics-wise. But...Marc was definitely androgynous, and it was not beyond the bounds of possibilities that his sexy little plea was exactly what it sounded like! How that occurred I was not sure; it had not been covered in our weekly dissections of The Naked Ape! But doubtless I would find out...

I had the single now to go jellylike over; how not to! The holidays were coming, and it was usual for parents (even mine!) to give us some money to spend on what we liked. Ideally they meant something unusual from the far off exotic coasts of Ayr and Devon, or the mountain regions of Cumbria though, not a small circle of oh-so-precious vinyl from Wilson Peck!

For once, whilst it was of course wonderful to be off school that summer, the old childhood freedom had gone, replaced by a deep longing for something I knew was there...only I did not know what it was.

For one thing, rock bands did not appear to tour in the summer. Perhaps they too had to go on holiday with *their* families, I thought miserably. Personally, I was off to the Lake District as usual with mine for two weeks, but now there was so much to miss!

For one thing, I had no record player to listen to my beloved music, although I *did* get to have a room of my own, albeit a tiny room with a sloping roof under the eaves of the rented house called Copt How; almost echoes here of The Cupboard under the Stairs... but at least my own space in which to snuggle on a floor mattress, reflect on the charms and assets of my Chosen One, and try desperately to tune in to Sounds of the Seventies, which was simply not going to happen because of all the beautiful, solemn, surrounding mountains.

It was no longer enough to be off somewhere new with my own family in the gigantic Ford Zephyr, terrorising other tourists who would be picnicking quietly somewhere when we all turned up and began a military-like operation to spread enough food for an entire homeless shelter out on the grass, proceed to cook up gourmet meals on a camping gas, go for really long, noisy walks in which one of us six would be in a bad mood throughout and not appear in the photos, and then have four or five really loud games of cricket in the lovely empty space provided now that we had driven all the other sixty-eight cars away!

I had always read books in which the Famous Five or the Four on an Adventure would have Ham and Turkey sandwiches and Lashings and Lashings of ginger beer. But there was no mention here of army-sized pans of stew and vast custard pies made from stolen duck eggs from local farms!

September came. After a couple more weeks of picking blackberries and various other wild fruit here and there on weekends and in the woods on weekdays, it was back to school, a hated place, but still...it brought me closer to the time when my favourite bands would tour again.

Not soon enough it was again the October break. This time I picked potatoes until my hands almost fell off, because I wanted something wonderful to wear for the next concert. My diminutive curly-haired Hero would be playing Sheffield again on October twenty third. We already had tickets.

Kim was really a rocker at heart, so it was to her credit that she came a second time to see T.Rex (the Tyrannosaurus having been permanently interred now beneath the Warlock's castle).

Most of the people at school jeered at us for this and various other digressions from the Done Thing in subtle, Grammar-school fashion, stealing their lines from Monty Python and Frank Zappa.

However; a little clique of new friends had sprung up around us; we were now approximately seven girls who liked Glam Rock. Elaine was crazy about Elton John, for instance, and even I had to agree that it did not detract at all from his very good songwriting and music to wear purple and orange spotted specs and eight inch silver boots. He just.....wasn't pretty.....

We all agreed to go later, when he would tour, and see Elton John with Elaine, however; our tiny group had to stick together.

So we were at least five now who entered the Hallowed Temple of Sheffield once again, freshly scrubbed from Spud Bashing, on a fine evening on October twenty third to see T.Rex once more.

But this time it was very different!

Someone was playing support, but the poor things had not much chance of appreciation, what with all the girls and half of the boys here spending the whole support band's set in the loos fixing their velvet pants, satin jackets and glitter to maximum effect and durability for what was about to come.

As the interval came and we gathered our droopy cotton hippie bags together in one seat ready for the charge to the front, I felt almost sick with nerves. Why it used to affect me so much I have no idea; it was as if I myself were about to go onstage. I seemed to align myself in some psychic manner with the fate of the band about to take the stage, as though I were responsible for their imminent failure or success.

And then they were on, and......CCHHHAAARRGGE!!!

We more or less ended up all together, but I and Kim were further forward and I wriggled under arms and through momentary gaps until I ended up right at the front. In this moment I realised that I belonged here for every future concert, forever, and indeed the Stadium gigs of the future decades never made me feel very much in comparison.

Here you were truly in the pit, no way to get out except until the end.

Here you got to see every pore, every bead of sweat, every flicker of expression on the face of your adored being and somehow like this they entered deep into you to imprint on you forever.

I think these small, intimate concerts were what inspired such deep love for the artists of these days. Seeing their faces, gauging their emotions, knowing they might be a little nervous, sending them encouragement.

If Marc Bolan *was* nervous you would never have known it. Such a tiny creature, but so perfect. He really was just so beautiful this close up as on TV or on an album cover. His pretty face was sparkling with glitter, and he himself sparkled with confidence, genuine happiness at our adoration and huge enthusiasm for his own music, his own abilities and his own flirty, pretty ways and performance.

He was at the very meridian of his career, he had just made it now to the summit, the zenith, but had not even rested on it. At this very moment he was a true star, shining at his brightest before the fog of criticism could even find him to begin to obscure his incandescence.

They played electric instruments now, and there were a few new musicians, but Mickey Finn still played mostly bongos and other percussion. The difference was that he popped out a lot from behind his kit now, shaking maraccas and singing along enthusiastically, his long hair swaying. He was also very easy on the eye, and this did not go unnoticed by us teenage crowd.

There were tears and sobs of adoration when Marc sat alone, cross-legged, though, to sing lovely ballads like Cosmic Dancer and Life's a Gas. He was a true Prince of Darkness, Romance and Fantasy this night. Alternately holding us in his palm as he crooned soft little ballads and making us scream as he picked up his electric guitar and flicked his hair, raining down glitter on us, he left the stage a hero who the Jeans Brigade at school had missed through their nascent bigotry, and now he would become one of rock's first and biggest early seventies superstars.

Tonight was a night that my dad could pick us up, so we quickly slipped around the back of the City Hall on our exit, since we did not have to run for the bus.

There were a little crowd of teenage fluffies around the backstage door, all relating their feelings to anyone who wished to listen. We were all connected by this amazing cloud of perfumed glitter, soft, sultry, suggestive seduction and fantasy worlds which made up the T. Rextasy experience.

No thrust-out crotches here, no traditional Lerve songs to speak of, no drunken killings in bars in Rio.

No, Marc Bolan had taken us with him to his ideal romantic place, a Gothic castle with a Dark Wizard, who was perhaps him, his diminutive, curly-haired protection offered nevertheless without question, and offered to slay dragons for us, afterwards sweeping us up into his arms and covering us with curly, glittery kisses...

His fans, us, right now, were pubescents and pre-pubescents for whom that was enough, and the right place to stop. We were too young, and essentially innocent despite The Naked Ape and Elaine telling us some 'facts', to need to go further than the sweet Princelike imagery he offered...

And then They came out of the backstage door. There was a flurry of movement and we all shoved out of the way the new friends we had been confiding in moments before, in order to reach the tiny, elfin creature flanked on both sides by two security people.

But they only had two arms each.

Mickey Finn passed by first, barely escaping with all of his long hair still on his head, and then Marc was hustled right past me. I simply put out my hand and touched the sleeve of his crimson velvet jacket, not grabbing, just laid my hand on his sleeve for a second.....then his corkscrew curls whirled over his shoulders, his brilliant, glittering warmth, his palpable aura and his gorgeous, genuine smile faded as he was bundled into the limousine...

"I touched his arm! I touched his arm!" I repeated, dazed, walking back to my dad's car with Kim and the others, since it was a multiple lift job for dad tonight (we still had that eight-seater-at-a-squash Ford Zephyr, which in retrospect my dad could have hired out to visiting rock stars...).

I do not know how many times I wore that paisley print silk blouse bought especcially for the show before I washed it. I used to sniff at it sometimes and swear I could smell him on it.

Somehow he was. Perhaps an atom of his DNA (neither word which I knew at this time) stayed on it, for slowly I was changing from a well-mannered, nicely behaved, 'normal' young girl, the apple of Daddy's eye (weird term!) into a rather.....different teenager. Perhaps a little of his fantasy world was being born in me.....

That winter I discovered Lord of the Rings for myself via the school library, and the secret world of which he spoke began to become more real for me than the everyday life I unconsciously sought so hard to escape. Wizards, goblins, elves and magic rings filled my waking and sleeping thoughts as slowly I began to see what Marc saw. His worlds.

I was now a disciple of The Warlock of Love.

CHAPTER FIVE – NIGHT FLIGHTS

Things were never the same again after the Arm incident. Something had shifted in the Cosmos, something had changed my world.

It was the accessibility, perhaps, of one of the most beautiful creatures ever to grace my Universe. The very fact that I had gone from reading about him, hearing his early style music, and then the later, seeing him live, seeing him on TV, covered in glitter, now a Superstar, seeing him live again, now at the height of his fame...and now I, little me, some schoolgirl from a small suburban town in Yorkshire, had laid my hand for a second on his arm, like some millisecond portion of a Michelangelo painting.

The tiny, fleeting connection had opened up a world of possibilities in me. My hair became more and more like his, my clothes more flashy, floaty, satiny and feathery, my make-up more colourful and glittery. Even my voice, my way to speak, aped his a little now, dropping it half an octave, and ironing out my Eyop Thee Yorkshire Lass tones, softening my vowels and making me say 'man' and 'cats' and 'cool' a lot.

My music tastes also became more and more diverse. I used to listen, as I said, to John Peel's Sounds of the Seventies, ten pm till midnight on weekdays, on a small orange plastic mono radio with one headphone, inherited from somewhere obscure. It was probably the most amazing, durable and informative piece of technical equipment I had ever possessed.

Now every night I lay in bed and absorbed music; sometimes I would be awake till midnight, sometimes I must have dropped off as early as half an hour into the show. I swear that sometimes I would hear tracks elsewhere which I recognised without ever having heard them consciously before. That is why I say 'absorbed', as I must have heard many tracks in my sleep.

And there surely was a lot of unusual new music coming up nowadays. T.Rex had been popular on the cult programme when they were just a young Tyrannosaurus, but as an electric Glam Rock outfit they were no longer of interest to the hosts of SOTS. But there were new musicians being played and spoken of with awe now, and their work was even more interesting to my blossoming adult tastes.

Usually it was John Peel's comfortingly monotonous voice over the airwaves; occasionally it was that of 'Whispering' Bob Harris, who also hosted The Old Grey Whistle Test, *the* cult music show to try and catch at ten twenty five pm every Tuesday.

Mostly I *was* allowed to stay up for the OGWT as I turned fifteen in the November of 1971. But there were disadvantages, usually that my father went out on Tuesday nights with 'Uncle' Don for a drink (or more). That was good, but he usually returned inconveniently around ten forty five to eleven pm whilst it was still running, since it finished at eleven fifteen.

I did not like my father when he had 'had a drink'. He was unpredictable in his moods at the best of times, and that increased in his 'drinking moods'. He could be anything from waspish and critical to soppy and sentimental, but the latter was no more reassuring than the former, as then he would babble nonsense, giggle at his own humour and take the piss.

He took the piss more and more lately, out of everything concerning the 'new me'. My hair, my clothes, the way I carried myself (rather gracefully I believe!) He seemed to find something to criticise in everything I said these days, not transferring his ongoing criticism from my mum to me but spreading it out.

From a very long distance of time now I see that the man himself is the problem, not those he criticised, but at this time I was a somewhat shy teenager with what appeared to be a contradicting tendency to attract lots of attention to myself by dressing, looking, and these days behaving like, as they say up north, 'a right weirdo', and constant blows to the confidence were not something I needed.

I guess also with hindsight...he was jealous!

One word indicating that I was watching something a) more interesting than him and b) unrelated to his tastes, and there could be anything from a sharp rebuke, to the TV being switched off and missing the rest of OGWT, so it was like walking on a knife edge every week.

However, it was worth braving the situation weekly for the wealth of information, new music and new glimpses of what our potential heroes actually looked like on this amazing fifty minute show.

Imagine, once again, teenagers of today who are hopefully deeply enthralled in this book!

No You Tube, no Facebook, Twitter, Instagram. No Google!!!!! No gallery full of downloaded photographs and music. No Spotify or Tumblr! Videos did not as yet exist!

Only these little fifty minute shows once a week, these late-night radio programmes when you had school next day.

No recording things for later.

Only, as Osho says, The Now! This moment! Forever! Miss it and you have no second chance!

One night in early 1972 I was ready to watch the OGWT, as we all called it, when Bob Harris announced that there would be a set by a new artist whose name I had heard here and there quite often lately; David Bowie.

I think he was among the many artists I had 'absorbed' in my sleep because later when I explored his music I recognised a lot of it. I had been listening out for him more of late, and was rather curious as to what he actually looked like; he sounded....somehow...both nostalgic for the past, and yearning for the future. Rather like I felt a lot these days...

Meanwhile, as I awaited this David Bowie's set with a kind of buried excitement, Bob played us a couple of random tracks, one as always with some flashing psychedelic screen accompaniment.

Then this man, this David Bowie, and his band, came on and sang a couple of songs.

I think my mum was waiting up for my dad that night as she often did, curled up on the sofa reading a Mills and Boon, or bustling in and out with coffee and snacks.

"Do yer want a coffee, love? Or a nice cup of cocoa...?" "No thanks...shush, mum!" I admonished affectionately, gazing at the television as this strange, slim, pale, almost anorexic and definitely androgynous (one of my oft-used Marc key words) man began to sing his songs...

Beautiful, haunting, somehow as vulnerable as though he wore his nerves, blood and veins on the outside, this David Bowie sang quite a jaunty little song, his feet tapping, hips swaying, a rather engaging way to smile, with a mouth full of big, crooked teeth.

Strange songs, about alien races, and people who were not themselves. Futuristic stuff, interesting, confusing, a wealth of emotions jarring in an alienated, non-belonging way.

Like I often felt! Not belonging, not knowing who was the 'I' my parents and teachers spoke about.

Not fitting in, not being understood. Teenage angst laid bare by a twenty-something man...which proved...it *wasn't* all automatically going to be alright when I left school and got a job doing whatever.

Here was someone ten years older than me, singing about it all, proving it even in his wistful expressions and winsome yet not-quite-happy glances at the camera.

Yes, he looked ill at ease. Shy and gawky somehow, despite his lovely face and outlandish space-age clothes.

David Bowie. So this was him, then...

It was not the type of look I had ever gone for, pale thin, blonde hair (then), especially *short* hair – it was kind of spiky on top and quite abundant, cut closer behind, a delicate-looking and vulnerable man. I had always been drawn to darker looks. Yet there was something here much more than simple physical attraction. And that *look* of his, like, 'Please like me! Please want me! Please love me!

He sported two different eyes too; one was light turquoise with a regular pupil, and one was a greenish colour with a large pupil. It was the first time I had ever seen that except in cats. So immediately, he was cat-like... And I love cats!

His teeth were large, wonky and a bit fang-like, but it made his smiles more genuine and winsome.

There was more music and chat from Bob Harris, then finally back to David Bowie, who now played his second song. Unfortunately my dad had now arrived home, and since tonight was the Sharp, Humourous Clifford, we got a little jibing going on regarding David Bowie's and his really cute guitarist's unusual satin and silk trousers. It was the Seventies and for one thing they were Not Flares and *definitely* Not Jeans!

For another thing...even a half-blind rabbit could see that they were unusually tight, and, well...*full.*

It was probably the last details, him being a father of a teenage daughter who was rapidly discovering new idols, which brought them to my father's attention, because he spent a full five minutes in and out of the room, trying to get a rise out of me. But tonight I kept quiet and didn't bite, because I *really* wanted to watch David Bowie and his band's set until the end and not risk him having an excuse to turn off the TV.

By the last song of this batch, my dad had gone to bed and I was able to watch in peace. And listen...

Another song, really haunting and quite long. I did not catch all the titles (one shot only!) but was pretty sure that if David Bowie was on the OGWT, he would be featured again soon on SOTS too; they appeared to run hand in hand as it were.

I went to bed and finished the night with the remainder of Sounds of the Seventies, hoping to hear a bit more David Bowie.

I would stay awake at nights from now on. And I would scan the music papers thoroughly. Because I had subconsciously moved up a level, found another singer and band which I really, really liked and really, *really* wanted to see live; David Bowie and his crew.

CHAPTER SIX - THE PIED PIPER OF BECKENHAM

A few things occurred during the coming months, one of which was that my school report was no longer shining like a star. My teachers berated me for fooling about in class, and then having the temerity to pass all the exams anyway.

What to do? I have a photographic memory and could study for an hour before an exam, devour everything and then, with my not-at-all-bad natural gifts with the English language, spew it all out again in a completely different order, style and format.

My father's response was to make a set of temporary 'new rules' for me as punishment.

A) he took the plug off the record player so that I could no longer play my music. B) he banned me going to any concerts for this time period. C) he would not allow me to make my

Marc Bolan hairstyle under my mother's hairdryer; he moved it up into their bedroom.

These punishments were provisionally in place for a month until I 'learned my lesson'. How well I learned it...well read on until the end of this book and judge for yourselves!

Incidentally, very recently whilst staying in Britain, I rented a room from a man who decided I used the tumble dryer 'too much' for my clothes, which we had no other way to dry in his damp house with its overgrown garden (plus, in England, in winter!). One day I came home to discover that he had taken the plug off the dryer. Within a week, I had a flight ticket booked...lesson good and learned!

So, back to now. About ten days of early spring of 1972 passed in this manner (which I spent a lot of at Kim's house listening to music!) after which I decided that life was simply not worth living, obviously!

Giving the matter some thought, and anyway being of the opinion, like any teenager worth their salt, that to hit the age of eighteen was terrible, the age of thirty unthinkable, I decided that an overdose of aspirin or some such was appropriate.

Being well organised, I wrote a suicide note, quite a lengthy one, a whole chapter in fact, and placed it under my bed ready for the next day's trip to buy aspirins...

I returned home from school next day, having forgotten all about the aspirins since the Sounds weekly music paper was out and some of my favourites were featured, including David Bowie! However, my mother was in a strange mood. "Your father wants a word with you..."

"What's all this, then?" was the statement which accompanied him holding up said suicide note. I was astonished that they had found it, but it appeared my mother had a penchant for cleaning under beds (see later) for no reason.

However, I coolly declared, "Well, you took the plug off the record player, etc etc..."

There was a subdued atmosphere in the house that night. Two days later, the plug reappeared on the record player. I was allowed again to 'freak out' my hair, and 'waste my money on rubbish' (records and concert tickets) again if I wanted.

Money...

Well, I had a new part-time job! Pocket money was now far from being enough for my growing needs in the form of concert tickets, fabric to make new clothes, and singles and albums.

I believe it was just after the 'not-suicide' event that I heard about it. It was a strange kind of a job, but quite alright as apart from the initial and then bi-weekly contact with the organiser, I was basically working alone.

Someone had told me about it at school, someone from one of the less wealthy amongst my friends. It was a job one of their friends or relatives had been doing, but now there was a vacancy as the person had found a 'real job'.

It was a simple arrangement if you were good with finance and counting of money, which I seemed to be. All I had to do was take around these pools coupons which people had subscribed to, and the money apparently went in part to cancer and polio research. I had a two week period in which to distribute them and collect the money, then I would meet at a set date and time with the organiser, he would collect the money and give me a commission.

It was just about five or six pounds every couple of weeks, but it was quite a large sum for me in those days, since 'spud bashing' was only once a year!

I used to do it at night, after school and 'tea', between the hours of about six pm and seven thirty, wandering around the streets up and down various paths, in my own little pattern, dressed in my by now handmade (well, machine-made, but by me) flowing skirts and this pair of wooden clogs which I had bought from somewhere, all the rage at the time! They were extremely comfortable, and the 'Crocs' of today owe their design to these really.

It was quite nice wandering once or twice a week around to various areas which my parents would have normally considered it unsavoury to visit. The most interesting place was down in the back of town, where the houses were in a long row but 'back to back', ie with windows only on the fronts of the houses, since the backs fitted snuggly against the other side of the rows. The railway tracks for the coal trains ran by here, since the coal pit of Manvers was a couple of miles distant.

The people here were, I suppose, quite poor, and definitely lower working class, but they were friendly and sometimes offered me tea or a cake or something. Usually I said no to the tea but yes to a cake. Strange, my mother was a very good cook, but these often shop-bought cakes were an exotic treat for me after years of home made ones!

In retrospect, I must have been as much of a strange sight then to these people as I would be now with my tattoos and dreadlocks. Flowing hippie skirts in bright colours, black velvet tops to break it up, beads well past my waist, those clogs, and in cooler weather, that Afghan coat over it all. Topped off with my ongoing Marc Bolan silver-gold afro of hair!

Well, that is how I was now financing my adventures until I could legally get a Saturday job at the age of sixteen. But that was some months away yet...

For now this would suffice. Now I had money for my adventures, and the restrictions of the 'punishment period' were over. The episode seemed if anything to have opened the doors to my freedom a little more; somewhere it had evidently been deemed that it was probably better to give me more freedom as a teenager, not less, for the moment. Perhaps the parents had actually done some talking, or listening, to other people!

Just as well, because within two weeks came the announcement that David Bowie and his band would be playing live at Sheffield City Hall in June, tickets on sale soon!

He also had some new songs, in fact a new album. It was bubbling in the music papers, on Sounds of the Seventies and a little news on the OGWT.

He was doing some interviews nowadays, and a lot of cute photos appeared of him in strange clothes and with either a kind of flat satin or velvet cap, or short spiky hair.

The interviews were also pretty outrageous ones. To my secret and inexplicable excitement, in one interview he declared himself to be 'gay'. We (the 'we of my little peer group) all knew David Bowie was married to Angie Bowie and had a young son called Zowie Bowie.

By now we also knew David's height, weight, hair colour(s), eye colour(s) and favourite food, since as well as the respectable music papers, we still crept into the newsagents and out again with Jackie and Mirabelle and such magazines hidden between pages of 'SOUNDS', bought just for this kind of riveting information...

But still...gay! Yes, somehow he *was.* We fifteen-year old kids *understood* with some weird inner certainty and a kind of all-seeing faith, that David Bowie *could* be both married *and* gay. Somehow...he was just *like* that.

I knew what 'gay' was, although the physical aspects of this still escaped me. But for some reason the figure of Lawrence of Arabia had fascinated me since I was thirteen and saw the movie, once with my family and then again with Kim, and I had bought the incredibly large volume The Seven Pillars of Wisdom and learned that 'Lawrence was a homosexual and had had a sexual relationship with his young Arab boy servants'.

For some reason this fascinated me. I had never, ever wanted kids. Being five years old and seeing my previously pretty, trim mother swollen and lumpen, breast-feeding my new twin sisters through these enormous glands, put me off pregnancy, childbirth and basically all things female for life. Here was a very simple, direct and uncomplicated alternative; two men together.

I *still* do not know to this day *why* I am attracted to this imagery, as I still am, since I am a female and can never experience it. But by now I also know that I am far from being the only female who feels this way.

And somehow, at the root of all this, is again...David Bowie.

I was sitting listening to the Ziggy Stardust album just now, in real time, and it suddenly hit me. Why we follow him. Why we who grew up with him in the Seventies are still mourning him in a way most of us do not even mourn family members. Why the sense of loss is so deep, almost six months later.

To understand, you had to be there, as they say. I bought Ziggy Stardust the day it came out. I got the early bus to Sheffield so that I would be in time for a copy. It was June sixth, 1972.

A few days later found me at the City Hall in front row seats with my best friend Kim. It was just a step up to watch the entire show from the front of the stage, and we did so, although it was only a small group of us who ventured to the front initially, the rest not following until near the end. David was at this stage another whispered word, another ripple in the pool.

It seems he had come to all of us discerning younger folk as a kind of rumour at this time. He was not famous, and not even well-known, but somehow *everyone* was talking about him right now. And after a few months of letting us feel the first vibrations of his it turned out limitless talent, here now he was presented to us as a headlining act who had never actually supported anyone in the sense.

And so he came onstage...

He was even more beautiful in the flesh. The pale, delicate young man who had graced the screens of the OGWT was in person still pale and still beautiful, but somehow much more real. His slim body was not as delicate and breakable as it looked onscreen but had a taut strength about it, and he whipped it obediently about the stage. He had, you could feel, enormous reserves of physical energy, and at the same time, a lightness on his feet which suggested dance rather than just music.

He was also...extremely sexy! I had not expected to feel this, but this slightly nerdy, mildly anorexic-looking young man with his odd eyes and wonky fangs...simply oozed sexual confidence! And therefore his appeal grew too in our eyes, as we began to see him through his own eyes...

He pranced and capered, and wiggled his hips and gazed into our eyes, not gazing off into space like most rock and blues bands did. He was more like a dancer, as I said, or an actor, or all at once since he was evidently a really talented musician too. There had only been a day or two in which to listen quickly through 'The Rise and Fall of Ziggy Stardust and the Spiders from Mars but already I had memorised most of the songs.

However, he played many others which I had never heard despite SOTS and OGWT. These were quite different to 'Ziggy', which seemed almost like a story, an album to be played in its entirety always. A lot of these songs were whimsical and strange and referred a lot of aliens, doppelgangers and truthfully, psychosis and mental trauma. Some of them, too, sounded as though they referred to homosexual encounters...

Well, now here was David Bowie, to tell us what they were all about.

And he did!

He informed, he withheld, he implored. Skinny, angular body clad in white satin, spiky hair like a red hedgehog now, an incredible jumble of wolf's fangs in that open, singing, smiling mouth, and those strange eyes, each with a different story.

He had the most enormous bulge in the front of those white satin pants, to which my eyes were riveted for a lot of the performance, especially as it was right in front of me!

Then he proceeded to enlighten us mostly twelve to eighteen year olds with one stroke as he drew his gorgeous blonde guitarist close and demonstrated various ways that men make love with only the guitar between them to keep it from being actual as opposed to implied.

By the time the show ended, I was again transformed, and had gone up another level. Now, even though I would still stay loyal to Marc Bolan as a backup for a little while longer, I knew in my bones that what I had just witnessed was on a completely different scale.

This man was...not complete yet. As in, his talent did not *end* with this style of music, for it quite evidently had not begun with such!

The variety of styles he had demonstrated throughout the show showed that he had the capacity for even more styles in the future. Although he was now performing 'Ziggy Stardust' in the main, his older material came from a wealth of different types of music. Which meant that his future music would be the same!

This man, this David Bowie...

He would never, ever bore me!

I went home, and directly that night I scribbled about it all in my diary whilst it was fresh, including the things he did with the truly beautiful blonde guitarist Mick Ronson. I included the phrase 'and they were very well hung!' gleaned directly from the Ziggy Stardust title track, and was quite artistically graphic in my descriptions, whilst my imagination ran riot!

My mother 'found' my diary whilst cleaning under the bed yet again and grounded me for a few days for 'making up a load of rubbish'. My diary was also missing...

After three days my father gave me back my diary. "I hope you enjoyed reading it," I flounced haughtily as I took it. "I haven't read your diary," he replied, to my surprise. "Just keep it out of your mother's way!"

There seemed to be some kind of unspoken bond amongst us teenagers because *no-one's* parents ever got to know for real what their children were seeing on various stages all over the country in 1972, and it appeared that even if we wrote it all down it was not believed! Let all the children boogie.....

Which brings me back to the album, Ziggy Stardust. For it was through this album more than any other ever by him or any other artist, that he seduced us, captured our souls and took us away with him on a journey from which some of us have never returned.

From the very first song he caught us, our minds, our imaginations. "Five Years" was written at a time when every few months came reports of possible nuclear war. Some of us teenagers really did think we might never live to grow up.

"Soul Love" elevates the power of love, but also separates different *types* of love, and confirms what we teenagers already know; that older generations just *don't* know the ferocity and depth of 'our' love. But David does.

"Moonage Daydream" has lyrics which confuse older generations but 'we' just *knew* what they meant. This song more than any other let us know that David's latent sexuality was waiting there ready to claim us when we would be ready...

"Starman" was the most obvious alienation of teenager from parents as he made it very clear that only 'us' (and him) would hear and see the Starman. And the double whammy was that he probably *was* that Starman.

"It Ain't Easy," the closer on side one, simply echoed the drowning sense of helplessness every teenager feels. 'Get some help when you're going down' was David holding out his hand, being that help.

Lovely "Lady Stardust, opening side two, was the yearning hymn to confused sexuality we all feel as teenagers. "I smiled sadly for a love I could not obey," showed that he felt it too.

"Star....." Well of *course* he was going to be a star! We, his fans, loyal now through every bone in our bodies, would see to that!

"Hang onto Yourself" and "Suffragette City" always made me as a fan feel that he is offering glimpes of other worlds, underground clubs, dark basements, crazy nightime streets, somewhere we had read of called Max's Kansas City. places we were not old enough to go to *yet*, but hang on in there, stick with him, and.....

Between these two comes the title track, the story in a nutshell of Ziggy Stardust and his band, which he had to break up in the end before they destroyed him. Retirement was more than a year away for him, yet although we fans were distraught when it happened, I think no true fan was shocked because he had already told us the story, explained the reasons why.

And "Rock n Roll Suicide....." I used to drink black coffee in my room at night so that I didn't sleep, chewing on my fingers, not wanting to smoke cigarettes but wishing that I did for this song. The desperation of being fifteen years old in small towns all over England was echoed here at it best as we realised that this rock star was not isolated up in his tower, he was with us, he could feel our pain. "You're not alone" embedded him in our hearts forever.

And so, with this album, he stole us, thousands of us. David Bowie, the Pied Piper of Beckenham, stole teenagers from all walks of life away from our parents under their very own roofs, through headphones in a million night-time bedrooms shared with sleeping younger siblings, without their knowledge or consent, without them even being aware of his presence.

After hearing The Rise and Fall of Ziggy Stardust and the Spiders from Mars, I was never the same. He understood, he knew. They did not. He was now the guide, the goal, the future. He had us forever in that moment, and reading the thousands of comments and grief-stricken notes and letters and photos and videos which pour onto the internet every day six months after his passing, he still does.

CHAPTER SEVEN – SCHOOL'S OUT!

Summer was truly here now. We sat at the edge of the sports field, watching with scorn as big, sweating girls and boys in navy blue shorts and light blue aertex shirts ran short spurts, long jogs, pole-vaulted, pitched heavy shots and discus (discii?) and collected points, prizes and praise from the heads of the teams and the sports teachers.

Scorn because...*we* had *far* more interesting things to talk about!

"Did you *see* Top of the Pops last night?!" Of *course* we all had; you would have to have been on holiday to Mars to miss this weekly Gift from the Gods to the teenage world!

"I know! did you see...?"

Yes, of course. We all had. We *all* had sat in our living rooms not daring to breathe, staring and staring, as the now flame-haired singer, whom I had seen live barely a month ago, flirted, invited, stared into our eyes and pointed at *us*, and told *us* that we only could hear the Starman. We only were invited to boogie, not our parents, older cousins, younger brothers, uncles...

And then he beckoned over his beautiful blonde guitarist, who we all knew by now was called Mick Ronson, and...SANG WITH HIS ARM AROUND HIM! ON THE TELLY! AND SOMEHOW OUR PARENTS HAD...SIMPLY NOT NOTICED!!!

This was the main topic of conversation; speculation abounded, obviously, about them having a lovely, androgynous, 'gay' affair, whilst simultaneously we weighed up how they would come on to *us...*

A few other topics were scheduled for the Glam Rock Clan meeting. One was...being asked by the Careers Master 'what we wanted to be when we grew up.' and supposedly having a sensible conversation about such with said Master.

My own meeting had gone thus:-

"So, Diana, what would you like to do when you leave school?"

I had privately told friends that I wanted something where I 'did a different job every day.' But to Mr. Deeley I simply replied airily, "Make made-to-measure jock straps for rock stars, sir."

For which my reputation swept back home in drag...

I was by now veering well and truly off the rails, the *direct* result of 'learning my lesson.' Constraint, albeit brief, had cut deep, and had the exact opposite effect on me.

Now I was becoming the most knowledgeable of all my peers...but not in the classroom, where I continued to astound with my results but where my methods of cramming before exams were not appreciated. No, my new knowledge was in the field of rock, and more especially, Glam Rock.

I dressed now like I was in some sort of rock band myself. Since my victory as such regarding the Record Plug episode, my hair and outfits had become wilder, my comments more succinct and sarcastic.

My school uniform, technically a grey sweater and skirt, white shirt, maroon and gold blazer and tie, now consisted of:- open-necked shirt to show off a jet choker found in some junk shop, tie loosened to show said choker, blazer always someplace else, as close to opaque black tights as was possible, grey sweater tight across my very good figure, and skirt halfway up my thighs.

With the halo of white blonde curls and eyes ringed with black to match the black nails, attitude of rock music expert and disdainful cool about anyone or anything not connected with my subjects, I looked, no doubt, like a teenage pre-Goth hooker!

The other subjects on the agenda on this school sports' day were mostly of other rock and Glam Rock outfits. By now there were a few more contenders to the throne...

Elton John was acknowledged to be 'a very good singer,' and we were loyal to Elaine's choice, but privately...well, let's just say that should he turn up to sweep her away, she would have no competition!

Far more interesting were some others. There was this weird duo called Sparks, two brothers, one easy on the eye, short like Marc with the same curly hair, but American, more pointily pretty and less truly beautiful, the other who looked for all the world like Lurch in the Adams Family! They were considered very cool, a bit arty, interesting.

Then there was Alice Cooper, another American who had long black hair and scary make-up, and went onstage with a snake and was supposed to bite the heads of chickens...or was it babies? Without a doubt, he had just won over every teenager in Britain with the anthem 'School's Out!' ('School's out for summer, School's out for ever, School's been blown to pieces...!' What's not to love?!). But despite his horrific appearance and crazy stage act, we did only see him as Hammer Horror, and no-one was even slightly afraid of him.

The last of these, though, Roxy Music, earned everyone's respect; as well as being quite a good-looking array of guys, they were genuinely making some seriously good music. Their single 'Virginia Plain' was now high in the charts, and news had already come that they would tour Britain the following spring, as would Elton John. 'We', since now we all *were* a 'we', a solid little group of seven or eight with a few shifting souls, would go and see both acts when the time came.

Summer holidays came. My family and I went to Ayr in Scotland. I bought my copy of The Slider by T.Rex as it came out, right there in Princess Street, Edinburgh. My dad must somewhere have a photoslide of me sitting astride one of the cannons at the castle, corkscrew curls sticking out and up, wearing some satin and silk outfit instead of Sensible Shorts (or Jeans) and clutching my new album in its bag for dear life.

Considering that my mind, if not my body, was already full of astride-the cannon type thoughts concerning certain Glam Rock musicians, the photograph was more than apt.

But that summer, like the last, was not the satisfying summer-stretching-forever that earlier summers had been.

I missed Kim, although our holidays were only for two weeks out of six; her family were not very wealthy and did not have a giant Ford Zephyr, or any car in fact, so they mostly went away for odd days on a bus. After I returned from Ayr we would wander around together, restless, looking for something we knew was not in our local area, no matter how hard we looked.

I missed bitching about people who had no musical taste with my new Glam Rock crowd. And I missed....so much I missed...what? A touch of a rock star's arm? A glance up from the front of the stage into the mesmeric, mismatched eyes of a man called David Bowie?

What I missed I could not exactly put my finger on. But *they* knew, these stars. They sang about it, that missing...whatever it was. And the reason we loved them most of all was that...they missed it too!

I was also studying in the school holidays this summer. So were many young students approaching their final year before 'O'levels. However, that is where the similarities stopped...

My subjects, you see, were extra-curricular, specialised, chosen as opposed to forced, and extremely absorbing...

After seeing David onstage, watching what he was acting out and showing us, I became extremely curious about these topics and began to checklist the references in his songs. I had by now purchased some of David's earlier albums, in particular The Man Who Sold The World.

This album was almost all about mental issues; psychoses, schizophrenia, seeing doubles of yourself and other such topics. But my very favourite track on the album was one which had caught my imagination when he had played it live, the very long, screeching guitar-dominated track which had several sections forming a kind of story; Width of a Circle.

Right from the first hearing I had known this was a song about a homosexual encounter, and a pretty hot one at that; "He swallowed his pride and puckered his lips, And showed me the leather belt round his hips…"

People are still to this day saying that the lyrics are 'ambiguous'. Well, not to this fifteen-year-old they weren't! It was perfectly obviously what was being said; I mean, how many ways can you take 'got laid by a young bordello?' I dived straight into the dictionary and ferreted out the meaning of the unknown word, and off we went on David's homosexual initiation journey!

So I was studying hard at David Bowie albums now.

The other one I bought was Hunky Dory. It was on the surface lighter and more upbeat. But there were a couple of tracks on it which were so strange…

The rather melancholy 'Quicksand' cross-referenced some names and words which sent me speeding to the library; 'Crowley' and 'Golden Dawn' being just two. It is such a strong song of spiritual quest that sometimes you almost feel like an intruder, as though David had really written it for himself and it just happened to end up on an album.

The other one was called The Bewlay Brothers and was one of the weirdest songs anyone has ever heard. Still today there are whole articles written about this song as listeners and avid Bowieites try to find new possible meanings. But to me…it is so obviously a fantasy story masking a reality, and simply to listen to the words and phrases without trying to dig too deep, it is clearly about someone very close to David, with whom he had a very deep, empathetic, and perhaps physical, relationship, who is now in some sense gone.

I was also studying the other artists David liked and spoke of.
Lou Reed and Iggy Pop were the most obvious, and of course
Andy Warhol. The former were American musicians, somehow
overlapping with Glam Rock but not exactly a part of it; Lou
Reed had been in a band called the Velvet Underground and I
managed to find a very cheap copy of one of their albums in a
second-hand record section. His music was kind of slutty and
languid and full, apparently, of references to drugs and
prostitutes and transexuals. So now I studied them...

Andy Warhol made movies about the same kinds of people
whom Lou Reed sang about. It was on our to-do list to go and
see one of Andy Warhol's movies if any ever appeared
anywhere. We thought we would not find the one of a man
sleeping for eight hours so interesting, but our goals were
Flesh, Trash or Heat, any of which we desperately wanted to
see. The 'we' here was just Kim and I; she was by now
specialising in art as I was in music, and found his strange
painting style very interesting.

There was another artist whom David spoke about in
interviews; the French homoerotic writer Jean Genet. It took a
lot of my Lottery Tickets income to find the money for these,
since they were in the most serious bookshop in town and no
chance that they would be discounted, but I finally purchased
two, Querelle of Brest and Our Lady of the Flowers.

They were translated into English of course; although French
was one of my subjects I really didn't see myself reading an
entire book in it.

Whooah! Here was all the information I had been looking for,
and more, as Jean Genet relayed in exact and graphic detail

with a pleasantly poetic style, exactly how boys did their 'thing!'

I pored over these books and by now had demanded a secret box to put them in. My father *did* get me a metal box, in fact he got one each for all of us. But...no locks!

Yet again, no locks for privacy, just like the bathroom, where I would wedge a stool against the door, and the toilet, which you kept your foot against.

What is it with British households even today that they do not have locks on the bathroom and bedroom doors? 'Health and safety', you might argue, but there was no such thing back in 1972.

No, I feel it is some characteristic of the British race that they feel that a closed door should be enough, like your word instead of a proper contract. The amount of times I had to yell 'oy' or some such exclamation in order to preserve my privacy whilst bathing, changing or washing. Never a moment's relaxation to really enjoy a bath or, these days, a shower.

Well, going back to Jean Genet...I actually found that the piano stool box where I kept my music, or Behind One of the Front Room Chairs, was a far more secure and less likely to be searched place than the so-called Private Box. Or, of course, Under the Bed!

So. Summer studies continued apace, and after a while I decided I enjoyed this homoerotic writing so much that perhaps...I would write my own story!

That, at least, was a simple matter back then; just a pen and a notebook. Or, notebooks, since I have a large scrawl. And the secretive, innocent-looking piano stool...

I had always written, my first 'novel' as such being produced at eight years old. It was about an Arabic boy and his horse, set in some desert somewhere, and was called Eldorado (the name of the horse here). My subsequent books were of the same type of subject matter, lions, cats and horses being the main stars. I wrote in complete secret wherever possible and never showed anyone, not even Kim.

But now I had a new subject...a homoerotic romance. People ask me often why today this is my chosen style in general when it comes to novels. Well, here is the answer!

I really enjoyed writing this now, and used my new knowledge gleaned from Jean Genet books to full effect, more or less stringing a series of naughty scenes together with some other action! I used to enjoy reading it back too, although in those days there was very little likelihood that this kind of writing would be published.

However, Jean Genet had got his past the censors...in the name of art and classics, but also, I suspect, because it was initially French and they are known for being much more open-minded. So...hope for me yet!

My private studies, my walks and talks with Kim and the playing to each other of our now almost separate styles of music with admirable mutual respect, and our separate but linked yearnings, formed the basis then of this summer of 1972.

CHAPTER EIGHT – TEENAGE WILDLIFE

There was a tingling, an undercurrent, this time as we returned to school in the autumn. It could have been partially explained by the fact that this was our 'O' levels year and our last chance to study really hard, heads down, so that we could achieve our greatest hopes (or more likely those of our parents.

But there was something else too, for we were teenagers now on the verge of adulthood, since sixteen heralded the legal right to do...quite a few things, learning to drive being only one of them.

There *were* a couple of girls here and there in the lower streams who had quite clearly done some of those other things. One of them used to tell us some details in the school breaks, a girl who I knew from the earlier forms before we elite were more stringently separated. She merely described the act as 'a lovely feeling, but it hurts ' though, a far cry from my Jean Genet books and even from The Naked Ape in informative terms.

The other one, though, Sue something, from just a couple of streams below us, did not return to school for the autumn term. Although just fifteen, she had 'got herself pregnant', a strange term since it is physically impossible.

I remember seeing her on the bus a year or two later with a tiny new baby, the first one in a pushchair. At still less than seventeen, her life choices and their obvious results were much more of a warning to 'be careful' than a million of my dad's words of advice to 'get myself a packet of pills', muttered gruffly once whilst I was helping him with the wallpapering in the front room.

Nevertheless, this new (for most of us) possibility was now there for us along with other choices we had to make.

It was never, as I said, of any interest to me to have children, and the local boys did not interest me at all, but ironically it *was* closer in my thoughts than I allowed anyone to know!

The other matters to occupy us all daily nowadays were, what subjects we would specialise in after this year, what colleges and Universities we wanted to attend, what-we-wanted-to-be-when-we-grew-up, and in my case definitely, which bands we would choose from a largish amount these days to spend our album and ticket money on!

I do have a tendency to be a serial monogamist at least mentally, as opposed to a polygamist, at this time limited to musical areas.

So by the time I was in possession of the new T.Rex L.P. through loyalty and first love for fluffy Marc, my deepest affections had now moved on to a certain singer with spiky red hair, a mesmerising vulnerability and a full satin packet...*and* his beautiful blonde guitarist. That I still counted as monogamy as in my eyes they anyway came as a set.

There *was* a third party to this scenario actually...

When we returned to school in September with the usual distaste and scorn combined with the pleasure of seeing our bitching friends again, it was to discover that there was *one* flower in the new term's impending garden of weeds; the school was being painted.

But this was no ordinary painter...this one had the face not only of an angel, but the face, almost to the detail, of our own (around seven of us) angel hero, David Bowie's beautiful guitarist Mick Ronson.

His name (the painter), we discovered over the ensuing weeks, which turned into months, was Dave.

So now we had a Dave to match the Mick he looked like...David and Mick, like our two heroes rolled into one!

We (Kim, Elaine, Margaret, Sharon, Karen, Sue and I) must have been a nightmare for the poor man, possibly combined with a dream come true. A whole group of girls who evidently fancied the arse off him! But we were schoolgirls for God's sakes, out of bounds, not yet even sixteen, all hair and legs and jutting breasts, and the poor painter *had* to basically ignore us or face real trouble.

He did smile at us sometimes; that was enough to bring on almost an attack of the faints; echoes of 'I touched his arm' here, as in the current absence of our real rock heroes, we imbued *him* with a little star quality too.

We would appear outside the classroom or by the fence he was painting, peek in, giggle, and disappear again. We would make huge detours between classes around ponderous science blocks when we were enrolled in music and art, just to catch a glimpse of his angelic face and lithe, tanned body (on warmer days he wore dungarees with no shirt!) for a moment. Dave-the-painter.

His hair was more of a dirty blonde as opposed to Mick's platinum, but sun would lighten that soon...

We didn't actually have that much else to focus on that winter. A few minor rock and folk and progressive bands came and went, sure, but none were of the calibre of my old love, Marc Bolan, let alone my new obsession, David Bowie and his Spiders from Mars, as the band was now called. Especially his *favourite* Spider, who now, in disguise along with his master, also frequented the pages of my new rude novelette!

I did go along to see a couple of bands, trying, I suppose, to get into the head-down, shuffle-feet, beardy vibe of Groundhogs and Captain Beefheart. Certainly my status with the Serious Prog Rock set at school would have risen.

I really *did* try... I even played down my glitter a bit and wore slightly lower shoes! Nodded my head appreciatively in time with the rhythmic beat, got down with the groove. There were even some of the Other Group at the City Hall for these, the old friends I had lost to the Bitch Queen Ruth. But she herself was now in another class and, it seemed, not interested in this type of gig, if any.

But although I tried my best, I just could not work out why in order to be taken seriously, a musician had to be plain, beardy, straggly-haired, shuffle onto the stage still tuning their instruments as though we were interrupting their rehearsals, sing with their heads down or facing off somewhere into the distance, drink Real Ale, and wear jeans and a lumber shirt.

What was wrong with being a musician *and* being beautiful?

Clean-shaven face, beautiful hair, skilful make-up, silk and satin clad, sweat just a light glow, beautiful body displayed in sexy clothes, and clear, moving, miraculous lyrics sung into your eyes, coupled with a little mime, a flirty smile or two and a little musical sex-play, were so much more my style.

I had given it a last chance. Now I quit trying to be one of the Cool crowd. It was not for me.

Spring came at last. March brought two of the minor greats in succession; Elton John played Sheffield City Hall on the ninth, Roxy music on the twenty-eighth.

By now I was sixteen and had a Saturday job as well as the mini-pools collecting one which I did on a couple of nights a week. Just as well, as the forthcoming months were going to be expensive!

But since my not-suicide, my parents had let up on the restrictions a bit, so on the ninth March we all trooped down to the City Hall to see Elton John.

I can never, even to this day, get into a gig, a play or a show unless I am right down the front. On this occasion the audience were not of that type so we were stuck in our eighth row seats until the encore. It *was* a great show, however, and he the consumate singer with his amazing songwriter Bernie Taupin, who popped up onstage near to the end.

It's just that Elton John...looks as he looks! Shortish, dumpy, speccy, balding despite all the efforts he put into making himself appear cool and outrageous. Not a sexy hairstyle or a lean, toned body in sight! Nor anyone lovely to play with... Ah, shallow me!

Roxy Music were a different prospect. For one thing the move to the front was instant, For another, there were enough of them to satisfy every type of taste, from Brian Ferry as the suave, classic crooner, through Phil Manzanera's Satanic good looks and Andy MacKay's boyish, besuited charm, to Brian Eno, one of the weirdest-looking men in rock.

The latter was evidently a very educated public-school boy who wore his hair both long and bald at the same time. His outfits were a masterpiece of high camp tight satin and silk pants, glitter everywhere and huge banks of feathers crowning his outfits. He was also a musical genius and was in charge of the newest of instruments, the moog synthesiser.

Eno was then the most popular choice for the thinking Glam Rock fan and we all professed to have a crush on him. Roxy Music were very adept at what they did too, and we had a great night right at the front of the stage.

But for me there was *still* something missing. There did seem to be something in me which responded only to the Call of the Wildest. Like a wolf pining for its pack leader, I awaited the arrival of the Alpha!

And he was coming...

The press were already building him way ahead this time. David and his band had released a single, John I'm Only Dancing, but although some small film of it had been on TOTP, David was apparently in America whe it was released and so the edge was not on it.

Now, though, he had a new album...

Aladdin Sane was if anything even more exciting in a way than Ziggy Stardust. It was certainly deeper and more complex by far, and more beautiful, with wonderful piano work. Now *that* would be worth learning the piano for, I thought, listening to the stunningly beautiful waves of arpeggios tumbling from the speakers.

It was also somehow a much more adult album than 'Ziggy'. Adult...and more sad. Nostalgic, futuristic, yearning and yet disappointed.

It was obvious to many of us teens that David was not that happy in America...but what a wonderful way to portray it!

The tour which would follow this album by about a month is always now referred to as the Ziggy Stardust tour. But really, it was the Aladdin Sane tour. The lightning-flash make-up on the cover of this album was to be the logo of this tour too, and, as it turned out...perhaps the sign of David Bowie himself. Forever.

I pre-ordered the album; in those days you did, since such things normally came out on a Friday for some reason, or at least into the stores then. I went to Sheffield directly from school, breaking my own rule of never being seen out of class in my uniform, and I went straight home with it and did not even bother to go anywhere else shopping.

I hardly ate anything for 'tea', so anxious was I to play this new jewel.

And it did not disappoint.

There were some tracks on the album which were so deliciously dirty that I could hardly wait to see them translated into a new stage show, especially Cracked Actor and Time, both of which contained very rude imagery and words.

He was coming soon. Touring Britain. He was coming!!

Now all that remained was the nerve-wracking experience of getting a ticket; I could not, literally, *bear* it if the show were sold out!

CHAPTER NINE - ROCK AROUND THE BLOCK

Once upon a time, before there was Online Ticket Booking...'

Exactly one year to the day of the release of Ziggy Stardust album and just a day short of my very first onstage encounter with the Starman himself the previous year, he was to play Sheffield City Hall again.

This concert was a *very* different affair to last year's. For a start, the build-up to it was intense. The musical press now carried articles and interviews with David Bowie almost every week. I cut each one out and painstaking sellotaped them into my scrapbook.

I watched the late-night TV show The Old Grey Whistle Test every week just to hear even his name, but there was not much coverage. Whispering Bob Harris did not appear to find David and the Spiders of as much interest as he had before when they were more of an underground act. The previous year's iconic Top of the Pops appearance had put paid to that once and for all. Now even some 'normal' kids at school appeared to have heard of him!

However, they were not the kids who got together spare blankets and kaguls and flasks and sneaked out of their parents' houses (following the Pied Piper again!) in late April to camp all the way around the block which housed the City Hall and its sister establishment, the *only* real record store in town to go to, and the agent for the hall's concert tickets, Wilson Peck.

This small store, with its hallowed basement from which you emerged looking a bit battered and hopefully clutching your ticket or record, is probably a furniture shop nowadays, its walls telling the stories of its past fame to bored-looking sofas and Queen-sized beds, but in those days it was the Temple of the Holy Grail for the Sheffield rock fan.

I went to my friend Kim's house to start the Camping Trip. Kim's parents were cool and liberal and friendly and warm and they knew where we were going and for what purpose. Her mum filled our flasks and made us sandwiches; I couldn't ask at home since my parents thought I was having a pre-O-level study and sleepover at Kim's house. We always began dodgy trips there, the same as when we had gone to Attercliffe Fleapit finally in late October to watch Andy Warhol's 'Trash', in more make-up than a pair of drag queens since we were then fifteen and the entry was eighteen. Luckily her parents did not own a telephone.

So then it was On The Late Bus (number 69, ironically) which took us to Sheffield. We walked up the long, slow hill to Wilson Peck with trepidation; would we be the only two idiots there, would someone chase us away, or would there be a queue halfway down The Moor?

We breathed sighs of relief mingled with envy as we reached the Hallowed Doors; there were two hunched humps, then one more, then two more; we were numbers six and seven in that line. But we were '*not* alone!'

As the night wore on the line grew, swelled to ten, then fifteen, until by midnight, when all the local transport had stopped and the North was sleeping, there were around forty people lined up on the pavement in the dark. Now our true vigil had begun.

At first we had chatted with our new neighbours. There was an edge to it all; we all loved David Bowie and there were already a few little Ziggys in the line, but at the same time here was our competition, the Other Ones whom we had to displace in order to reach the feet of the Master. We didn't look at it like that then, but we were all as ruthless as business tycoons and prepared to fight like wildcats for the last ticket no matter how nice the new friend we had made ten hours ago appeared to be.

I can never sleep properly unless I am lying down fully covered up, so I spent half the night walking up and down to the toilets in a sort of road-crossing subway section in the centre of town, partially to have a piss and drink from the taps (it was the seventies, we didn't need bottled water then) and partially to warm my semi-frozen fingers under the hand dryers. Another aside; in those days the toilets were open for anyone all night; no-one felt to lock them in case of theft or vandalism. What exactly *can* you steal from a toilet, anyway...?

As the dawn broke I rose stiffly from a shallow sleep and went to visit my by now good friends The Underground Toilets again, this time armed with toothbrush and paste, mascara, deodorant, some cheap cologne I am sure, and a change of clothes, because now it was almost time to show yourself as a Proper Bowie Fan.

My hair was never cropped in his style or dyed his colour. I still had natural long silver-blonde hair, still made it into a copy of Marc Bolan's lovely, coveted curly dark locks. The result was....well, you could spot me for miles anyway.

And my clothes......my father had bought me a sewing machine when I was thirteen so that I would at least not keep making weird clothes by hand; now I made them on the machine, but despite his sending me to sewing classes to 'learn to make things properly' my current style was no less weird. I used to buy the fabric and trimmings that caught my eye first and decide what would come from them afterwards.

It was all topped off, especially but not exclusively in winter months, when I also had the Afghan coat, like now for instance, with any loud sequined items, long trailing strings of beads, large fake crystal pieces, feather boas and bits of ratty fox furs and other such treasures which I could find in Barnsley market.

I emerged from my toilet lair and returned to The Queue. By now the other overnighters were crawling out of sleeping bags and from under blankets and coats, Ziggy make-up smudged and Ziggy hairdos limp, everyone of us crawling like zombies towards any kind of refreshment place we could find open, murmuring "Coffee, coffee," as opposed to "Brainz, brainz....."

A couple of coffees from the local Wimpy bar later, and I felt much more human. Now was the time to socialise, and check out the competition.....

One of my best finds in the now very long queue, which stretched way past the front of the City Hall and curled around it comfortingly, was a long-back best friend of mine from Junior School, Simon Palfreman, who had spent the last five years at a different middle school in a neighbouring town. We renewed our old acquaintance right then and were firm friends onwards until my departure from the north to London a couple of years down the line, after which time, tide and on his part, college, slowly drew us apart.

The thing with Simon was that a) I had not known he was into David Bowie, b) his Ziggy haircut suited him well and c) with my new-found Bowie experience I knew with one glance what he had not told anyone yet; that he was gay. He came out shortly after seeing David's performance in June.

The time was ticking on, the moment getting closer to those doors opening. By eight forty a.m I was back in my place, number six in the row. Kim was technically number seven; a loyal friend, she knew my love of David was greater than hers and if there had been one last ticket she would have made sure I was the one to have it. Her great love was still Paul Rodgers of Free.

Tension mounted as the staff arrived and unlocked the doors, let themselves in and closed them again! We all let out groans of protest, but the poor devils probably did not know what to do, having got up that morning ready for a normal day's work and instead having to face up to more than two hundred eager (obsessive) fans right in their face as soon as they arrived

It was past nine now, almost ten past...

And then the doors opened.....

CHAPTER TEN - LOVING THE ALIEN PART ONE

The sixth of June crept closer. Although Kim and I had been to a few concerts this year already, they were low-key affairs apart from Roxy Music and Elton John; rock bands, progressive/blues bands; tatty jeans and long-sleeved star t-shirts a la Paul Rodgers would suffice. But not for *this* concert!

I found some fabric which was patterned fit to give a Harlequin a heart attack, and sufficiently removed from denim to alienate me from most of my class at school, who already thought me over the top with my fake-leather fringed waistcoast, adjusted by me from a plain one where I had chopped liberally and confidently into it with scissors to create the cowboy-style fringes.

I sat and sewed this new silky, satiny stuff into pants with tiered ruches which flowed to the tops of my eight inch platform shoes, and covered an also hand-made, non-matching top with hundreds of small sequins. There! I would now do my idol justice! It was not like any clothes he wore, but it was glam, satiny, and my own creation. So actually, it *was* his style, for David Bowie is exactly that...your own style!

We filed into the City Hall along with other friends. After all, from our all-night vigil, Kim and I had been allocated tickets in row X; we had all discovered that the majority of seats in the house had been block-bought ahead of us by some invisible demons. However; it was *still* downstairs. There was still a chance to reach the stage. The thought of being up in the Gods, so far from him, would have been too awful to contemplate.

Some opening act was on, in which I went repeatedly to the toilet to try to pee ahead since once he came on..... I checked my make-up; I was never big on lipstick, but the thick waterproof mascara, turquoise eyeshadow and matching glitter were a *must!*

I am quite small, but good food and plenty of tree-climbing as a child had made me a strong, lithe creature. As the last few minutes of the interval crawled by, the tension in me mounted and mounted.....there was never a drug made in this world which could have taken me to the heights that those last few minutes did. I was on a knife edge, the opening music began.....

.....and I, all five foot three and a half of me, raced down the full length of the City Hall aisle in those eight inch platforms without a word or a backward glance to my other friends, only barking 'go' to my bestie, dodging around others, pushing through the last few rows.....a bouncer attempted to stop me but I made a running dive under his arm and.....

We were there! Right at the front of the stage! I had managed it, I think, before the poor suckers with genuine front row seats, who had probably sat in their houses waiting for their postal tickets the agents had stolen from us, had even stood up. Along with forty or fifty really hard core fans (probably the same ones who slept out that night with us) I now formed part of the Front of the Stage elite, the ones that the bouncers didn't even try to move; they were now occupied with keeping back the larger crowd who had gone 'what the fuck?' and then trailed after us.

It still makes the hairs stand up on my arms when I see the Pennebaker movie and know that yeah, that bit of Clockwork Orange and those few bars of Hang Onto Yourself heralded the arrival onstage of the greatest genuine superstar of the seventies.

And I had liked him before all this, seen his potential, listened in awe under the bedclothes to Sounds of the Seventies on my little mono radio headphone to tracks from Hunky Dory and the Man Who Sold the World, bought Space Oddity album and wondered sadly who was the girl who hurt him so much, and last year had Seen Him Live when all these *new* fans, these Ziggy-wannabees, were still saying 'who?'

Then he came onstage.

He was wearing a long kimono. His red hedgehog hair was longer now, swept behind his Vulcan ears, prettier, sexier. He had more make-up on, and it was much more professional, culminating in a round shiny sort of disc in the centre of his forehead. His skin was as usual as pale as milk, his lips glossed the softest shiny pearl pink. His eyes.....the make-up was exquisite, but more so was the calm love and beauty with which he gazed on us, the crowd.

His crowd. His own children, come to boogie. That which he had foretold, had created, had come to pass. The Starman was here now. He had landed, and we had all come to pay homage.

His band were in tight, glittery form. Mick Ronson looked less pretty and more aggressively beautiful now too, his make-up thick and viciously Gothic in contrast to his lovely, masculine body and gorgeous arms with their light tan and little blonde hairs. When it came down to it after all...he looked nothing like Dave-the-painter!

He oozed confidence on this tour, whereas on the previous one he had looked rather taken aback by a) finding himself onstage in full make-up and drag, b) being backed into corners, grinded on and felt up by a grinning David and c) amazed at how much girls love this sort of thing!

And then there is David.

His body is lean and angular. He is a little tall but not excessively so. His skin is pale, almost luminous. He has shed the white kimono now for a smaller version, which is just really a little top and very brief shorts.

He is right in front of me. The City Hall is a small venue, the stage is low enough to rest your elbows on. I could touch him if I wished at some points. I don't unless his fingers trail out on purpose; there is a kind of unwritten rule that those of us who make it to the front are as responsible for the safety of the star in front of us as the paid bouncers.

I am at this point sixteen and a virgin, and I have never seen *so* much of a man's body before. Yes, I have been to the swimming baths, but they are *boys.* Yes, I've been on Saturdays too, but they are just.....men. They are not pale, slender, luminous gods clad only in by now a very brief romper suit with bunnies on it, and they are certainly not barefoot in public, right in front of me.....

David does not shimmy his crotch in your face. He does not place his hands suggestively on it or thrust it out in a parody of sex.

What David Bowie does is to place all the goods nicely on the table, stand back with a little smile and let you admire them.

Just a little wink, a lick of his lips, a head-toss, a raised eyebrow, is enough of an aside to whisper "and by the way, if there's anything you see that you like the look of....."

So you, as a still-semi-innocent teenager can gaze up at him and really admire those goods without worrying that he's going to come along, stare hard at you and say, "Well? Do you want this or what?"

He's not. He will let you pick and choose just as long as you want. That is his gift, and that is why he attracts so many young people of both sexes.

Something about those bare feet.....so poignant and beautiful, long, pale toes. I had never seen an artist or band perform in bare feet before.

Something about the way he put it all on the line.....so vulnerable, so passively visible, so easy to reach out and hurt him, he is so available, standing almost naked and barefoot on the stage.....I wonder if he even knew the immense protective instinct he invoked by presenting himself to us with all his beauty and all his flaws laid out before us?

His stage act was much more fluid, less jerky and experimental than before. He played quite a lot of the songs he had before, but also lots of the new album, Aladdin Sane, which of course I already had.

I loved the songs on this new album. 'Ziggy' was wonderful, and Man Who Sold The World has to be one of my favourite albums of all time. Hunky Dory and Space Oddity showed so much versatility.

But Aladdin Sane was...such a *grown up* album somehow. All yearning and emotional and romantic and despairing, with its incredible piano work and disjointed, disillusioned vocal style, as though David had seen too much on his last trip to America and come back to tell us of it.

The edgy, nervy shrieks of 'Watch That Man,' Panic in Detroit' and 'Drive in Saturday' took us to the edge of our David's experiences in the big cities of America which we had only heard of.

But it was the double whammy of 'Time' and 'Width of a Circle' which had us staring up at him in amazement as he proceeded to simulate acts with Mick Ronson which I had begun to regard as pretty much normal after reading some of the Jean Genet books.

At one point he curled to the ground in front of me and 'got raped' by Mick Ronson, who ground down on him with that new confident aggression as his amazing guitar howled out stallion-like screams, getting his revenge for a bit earlier when David had grabbed his buttocks and, to our astonishment, proceeded to fellate the blonde man's guitar.

And throughout it all, still David has the face of an angel, as though, yes, all this sexual stuff is happening to him, being thrown at him to experience, but somehow he himself remains an innocent in all this, almost a victim...

There are some quiet pieces in the show too, a couple of songs which he sings sitting on a stool with Mick Ronson only beside him.

I *do* love them together. I don't *think,* despite my wishes, that they are an item, but they are an amazing musical team, fitting together like two parts of some extraordinary new musical device which only works when both parts are installed. David and Mick, Mick and David.

And yet...although I love him a lot, Mick Ronson alone onstage is not enough. There is a long pause when David leaves the stage during one song and Mick has some kind of space-age fight with Trevor Bolder, the bass player. But although it is initially great to hear Mick's guitar solos, there comes a point at which you get tense, nervy, edgy. Like...where is He? Where has he gone? When will he come back? *Will* he come back...?

And when he does...we all cheer so hard it is as though David has been on holiday for a year and has now returned.

But when even Mick Ronson leaves the stage and David alone occupies a solo stool and sings another Jacques Brel song, My Death...a song so haunting...

...he could continue to sit there all night alone, playing us songs and staring winsomely into our eyes, and no-one would even remember there *was* a backing band.

I am not doing his band, especially Mick, any injustice or showing any disrespect here. Only that...four men were on the stage tonight – perhaps five; I think there was a piano player too this time.

But only one of them can leave and you feel the light of the world has gone out.

And that is the mark of the true star.

All too soon it is the encore. David swanned back on in another revealing outfit, with a red feather boa initially around his neck.

Halfway through the song, a large feather fell off it right in front of me. I picked it up and gazed guiltily up at its owner; could I keep it? But the man before me with the pale skin and the long, beautiful toes simply curled his lip in a little grin, and I tucked it hastily in the tiny banana-shaped bag which held just my house key and money. It later became the first feather earring I ever made.....

My dad sometimes used to come and collect us from concerts if they were on Tuesdays or Fridays, his nights out with his friends. On those occasions we could hang around the backstage door for a glimpse of Them (whoever the night's

Them were) leaving. But this was not either of those days, so the moment the concert ended I collected my friends, who, except for my faithful Kim, were scattered around in the crowd, their possessions scattered elsewhere, and we legged it the ten minute run down to the bus station to catch the last bus at eleven fifteen.

I was quiet on that bus. I had been in awe of him before, loved his music, yearned to see him in concert again. But now.....something had happened. This time, with his almost-nakedness and his beautiful bare feet, his deep happiness at seeing his fans and followers at last exactly that, all his, and his absolutely riveting performance and star quality, he had touched my very core with his being. A little piece of his feather boa was in my bag, and a little piece of his soul was in mine.

CHAPTER ELEVEN - LOVING THE ALIEN PART TWO

Before the June sixth concert came the announcement of a few extra gigs on the 1973 tour. One of them was in Doncaster, more or less equidistant from our house with Sheffield, in a different direction. I had had a Saturday job for the last eight months now and could afford my own tickets, so I happily applied by post for this one since it was an unexpected gig. Shortly, too my tickets (one each for me and Kim) came in the post and I paraded them happily around.

But a few nights after the Sheffield concert I was speaking about it and my dad responded, "You're not going to *that* one." "What? What do you mean?" "It's at the *Top Rank* Club," he snorted through curled lips as though he spoke of the local Satanist Church. "And it starts *late!* And there's *alcohol!*"

He had no idea about Kim and I's excursion to Seedy Attercliffe for an Andy Warhol film, and no amount of "But we won't drink, we just want to see David Bowie!" would sway him. With hindsight I wonder if any of the press on My Hero was starting to filter through to the parents.....?

However, it was true, we did not drink and we only wanted to see David Bowie. It did indeed start at ten thirty pm, that was the time David would be going onstage, not coming off it as was the norm. But really truly honestly...we only wanted to see David Bowie!

That clamp-down on my concert-going and lack of trust in me would finally do what perhaps he had feared; it made me much more determined slightly further along the line, and since he didn't trust me.....might as well go ahead and do what he thought I might do.....and more.....

But that's another story, for now...

It did, though, change my approach to problems. No possibility of using the main door? Then find a side door!

Right now, I had this problem to deal with; no David Bowie. And there was no way in the world that he was going to come to Doncaster and I would not see him!

The twenty seventh of June dawned bright and sunny, as British summer days rarely do. School-wise, we were in that strange period of post-'O' level inactivity where we had lots of spare time to not study, not play sports and go on Geography Field Trips with the school to the local sewage works. Right, yeah.....

I had already done a 'posh-voice call-up' to the only two decent hotels in the area and knew which one they would be staying at. So then it was just a matter of pretending to be going to school in my uniform, racing across the fields to Kim's house and changing clothes.....

We were four girls since Kim's friends Sue and Karen wanted to come. They had been at the concert in Sheffield with us a couple of weeks before, along with a couple more people, including Simon.

We had the usual changes of buses before we reached Sheffield and then the long walk up to the Hallam Tower Hotel. It was around eleven thirty am when we reached the hotel and nervously approached. No buses, no limousines. Madame Diana went to check at the reception if 'Mr Bowie and his entourage' had yet arrived; no, but they were coming "about three pm".

The hotels never used to turn a hair. Perhaps it was too new a thing for them, this hotel-hopping by small groups of teenage girls. I have no idea how it would be now; I am sure they would not have the same tolerance of us that they had then.

We made a little 'camp' at the top of the drive where it bent around to the front of the hotel, found a bit of shade and grass to sit on there. And so, with minimal conversation except for a start upwards every time a vehicle approached the hotel, we waited.

And waited. It was actually *hot,* in England, in summer! Nowadays I probably would not think it so, it was perhaps about twenty three degrees, but certainly fine weather for Waiting for the Man. Men really; we were as excited to see lovely Mick Ronson as we were David.

They let us use the hotel lobby toilets and I popped in there every hour or so to freshen up. Around two forty-five pm I went in for a last pee and a spray of the best perfume I could find. Again tension was mounting and my mind was beginning to go blank as adrenalin built up and I began to focus solely on the task in hand...

At three fifteen a huge tour coach approached the hotel.....was it going to pass.....no! It slowed and gently slipped up the side drive and.....

I had made no plans. No idea what I was going to do. I had no merchandise with me to sign, no autograph book. The coach braked to a halt and *people* got off it.....

I was not aware until afterwards that one of my friends took a photo. It shows me standing to one side near the coach, tall in my seven inch black platform shoes (not the eight inch fake wood ones) and a long, skinny halter-neck dress I had made from some black, shiny fabric patterned with weird, colourful abstract lines and crosses, blonde hair in a long halo of curls, face turned to the also-blonde man who was smiling into the camera.

I was staring at him in awe. "A think yer beautiful," were the first words I ever uttered to Mick Ronson, who was indeed that.

And then my whole world changed in an instant as he didn't give me a funny look or a sneer, didn't shrug or smirk or just walk off.....

All in one smooth motion this gorgeous fellow-Yorkshireman put his arm around my waist, smiled his beautiful, genuine smile and said "A think *you're* beautiful too, love," and simply walked me into the hotel lobby alongside him.....

Perhaps if I had not been with friends that day I might be a different Diana writing you a different story. I'll never know.

Mick Ronson was certainly a very smooth, fast mover! We were already crossing the lobby, definitely on the way to the lift, and I...was just floating along, decision subconsciously made...

But.....

"Can we av yer autograph?" suddenly came a rather desperate cacophony of voices from somewhere in the background.....

Oh, Damn!!! I'd actually forgotten.....

So then it was autographs (mine on a rather grudgingly-given page taken from Sue's book) and some chat, and in the middle of all this.....

"He's here!" shouted someone from our group, and I was whirled outside again with the mini-tornado that was Sue and Karen, who were now about to meet their hero...

He had come in a limousine. The doors opened, the driver got out of one side.....opened a door...

And then everything died away, as he stepped forwards, pale skin looking vulnerable in the bright sunlight, hair as red as ever.....

And I looked into his eyes. And caught my breath...

There really were two different eyes. You couldn't see it so much at the concerts because of the lighting, but here, in the sun... Really, one light blue one with its small pupil, and a greenish one with that large pupil, and they both look at you at the same time, and each one has a different agenda.

They gleamed slightly as they looked into mine, curious, wary yet friendly, almost predatory.

Autographs and photographs were always a by-product of the meetings for me. It was *them* I came to see, to meet. My friends would move towards them wanting *something,* but I always wanted most of all to meet them, know their minds. I could have stood thus, gazing into those eyes forever.....

I suppose Sue and Karen made their moves then; I cannot remember. The driver or bodyguard or whoever came a little close as they began to ask for autographs, but David was not fazed by such a small group of girls and he made a small nod to the other man, who stayed nearby but let David mingle freely with us.

"Let's go into the hotel," he said gently; he was not one to stand out on the driveway getting baked by the sun.

Once inside, he moved into an area near to the reception and smilingly took the autograph books from the others.

Much later I heard stories that he said Ziggy as a character was taking him over, that all the fans thought he was Ziggy

Stardust and not David Bowie. He even told people that he *let* Ziggy do interviews for him, meet the public.

But David Bowie was the person I met now, a musician and performer, a beautiful man in his mid-twenties, a little tired from touring, sure, a little surprised at being waylaid en route to his afternoon nap probably, but nevertheless, an English man, somewhat alien-looking because of his pallor, and with incredibly strange eyes, but, David Bowie, not a character called Ziggy Stardust.

Perhaps, straight out of the limousine, not expecting anyone, he had not any time to slip into a character. I don't know. Perhaps we were incredibly lucky then!

Quite tall – even in my seven inch platforms I looked up at him (he had heels on too; it was the Seventies; we wore heels in the bedroom!). He was lean and angular, but not delicate at all; his body, as I had also noticed onstage, although possessing a remarkable vulnerability, was physically strong and toned, the body of a runner or a dancer perhaps, as opposed to a sportsman; despite its leanness, you sensed an immense strength and control.

He was gorgeous, like an exotic bird or animal, pale skin, red spiky hair, mismatching eyes, long, artistic fingers, honed, angular limbs in some less-than-concert but definitely more-than- street outfit, some kind of dungarees off one shoulder, and a stripey t-shirt or shirt.

He spoke like a London Lad, sharp and cool and edgy. He lit up a cigarette whilst we were surrounding him like puppies, trying to snuggle into him without appearing to touch him. "Do you smoke?" he asked, ready to offer one if we did. "No!" I at least replied, wide-eyed. "You shouldn't! Are you coming to the show tonight?"

At that I almost wailed. "Av got a ticket but mi dad won't let mi go!" He turned to me with that nose-wrinkling grin. "You should come," he suggested.

Yeah, but I'm just sixteen and have nowhere else to live.....

Well, I had a pen, but no paper; Sue had unaccountably now no spare pages in her book. "Come on," joked this beautiful man with his red hair and strange eyes and really gentle manner and more big crooked teeth than it seemed possible to fit into such a perfect mouth, "what have you been doing all day, no paper?"

"Waiting fer you," was my rather weak reply.

"I can sign your arm...?"

"It'll wash off!" I responded in a desperate voice. "But you could sign it as well...!" I brightened.

Then he rescued me. "Ask the desk for some paper," he suggested. "Come on, I haven't got all day," he added, grinning again.

"Yer'll wait, won't yer?" I squeaked up at him. Big eyes at him in case he would evaporate, then I scurried over to the reception desk, and back again clutching a small piece of paper.

I *always* had a pen, though. He used said pen then handed it back to me, smiling slightly.

Our fingers touched! His were incredibly soft. Mine were probably as attractive as a truck-driver's from constant piano practice and climbing trees.

"I like your hair," he remarked. "Nice colour." "It's natural," I stammered out. "Come to the show," he repeated, and with that he drifted off to the desk and shortly away to the lift.

I broke down into unaccountable sobs as we descended the drive which had accommodated us all day, murmuring "I love him!" However, although Kim was her usual stoic, helpful self, I could feel poisonous darts emanating from Sue.

They were closer friends of Kim than me. Sue had a blonde version of a Ziggy haircut, Karen a brown version.

There is a moment when you realise that you are.....how to say this nicely.....better-looking than your friends. I had always thought I was rather strange-looking, blonde and rather wimpy. My father had never been very encouraging there either, always ready with a put-down. And now.....first Mick, then...

I think it was the 'hair' thing more than anything else with Sue. I mean, he hadn't mentioned *her* hair, and she had gone to all the trouble.....

But then, mine was in a different style to his, it was if anything a similar style but different colour to that of his old friend Marc Bolan. I just knew somehow that David would like people to have their own style...

I kept staring at my little bit of paper and wondering what my dad would do if I just.....

"Come to the show....."

However, it was still early days for me and my complete rebellion would not come until more than a year later.....

But that's another story!

CHAPTER TWELVE – REBEL REBEL

David had spent one more week on tour with his Spiders from Mars and then on the third July rather dramatically decided to retire from touring forever!

I hoped it wasn't something I said...

In all seriousness even then 'we in the know', ie obsessive teenage fans, knew via the music press within a week of his announcement that David Bowie was already scheduling a new album, although 'new' was pushing this a bit. David's next offering was to be an album of cover versions of Sixties' hits.

It was our beloved David Bowie so we would all go and buy it faithfully, but covers have never been my thing and sixties music ditto, so I eagerly awaited my heroes having a rest and then coming back with their latest projects.

We already knew, too, that Mick Ronson would begin touring in the winter as a solo artist, since he had told us even at that meeting that he would be back 'soon' alone.

We had liked each other. I knew it. Something had clicked. I had privately decided.....to turn up a bit early for the next concert, and without my friends in tow this time. Already the worm was turning.

However, that was in the future, probably as late as next year. Right now...life dragged ahead as I could see no David Bowie tour on the horizon, not even in the autumn. Marc Bolan and T.Rex were also not touring in the near future; my little curly elf prince was trying to break it in America, Japan and Australia now.

I was sad in a way about David and Mick. I knew that Mick had plans to tour solo, but since David was supposed to have retired, who knew if he would ever play with Mick again? I think Mick had no idea either...

Somehow I felt let down. I had wanted this tour of theirs to last forever; it was truly the best, most inspiring set of concerts ever. I was not stupid; I did not think that David Bowie was Ziggy Stardust, and probably he would have become sick to death of playing the same set for another year. But...

In retrospect he could have done nothing more successful ever in his life than that retirement concert. For it was like serving an amazing meal in which you have a starter, and then a main course, are anticipating a wonderful dessert...maybe liquers, Irish coffee and cheese...and then halfway through the truly delicious main course someone comes and takes your plate away!

Forever and ever you will remember that meal, the one you never got to finish.

Well, my delicious meal was now off somewhere in France recording this Pinups album, and we were finishing the last weeks of the school term in this strange way of not needing to be at school all the time, supposedly studying in our spare time, taking the odd exam and so on.

There were also some school trips to go on. But these were not like the ones we went on in younger days. These were called Geography Field Trips. I don't know why we had them, because very few of us were taking Geography in the following term; I certainly wasn't! I had had a French pen friend for a while in slightly younger days, and then a Philippines one who spoke French, and for some time I had thought therefore that the Philippines were near France!

Well, one of these Field Trips was to the local sewage works, as I mentioned earlier. The most useful thing I discovered there was that there was a huge vat of cyanide!

The second one of these, though, was to Mam Tor in Derbyshire. This huge outcrop of a hill had a long sloping back and a bare, very steep front which looked for all the world as though someone had taken a bite out of it. I guess we were supposed to learn something from this trip, but for me I was just excited to climb it!

I had some leather sandals rather than 'good walking shoes' like the other girls. I had been brought *up* on good hiking boots and the like, what with my father's constant wishes to spend the holidays – all of them – climbing mountains. I liked climbing mountains, but always it had to be such a military organisation in our family! Now here was a chance to do it my way, and no-one to stop me climbing Mam Tor in my bare feet!

And so I did. On the early part of the climb we were the same group who had met David and Mick, plus a couple more who wanted to hear about it. So somehow in my mind, Mam Tor and the climbing of it has always been associated with David Bowie!

Perhaps it is somehow...he did write a song, much later, in which were the words 'Elvis (with whom he shares his birthday) is English and climbs the hills...'

News *was* bubbling that Lou Reed would play a tour of Britain in the autumn. I did like Lou and his music, but I didn't feel the same way about him as I did David and Mick... however, he was some kind of connection to the Master.

Always 'David and Mick'. Always together in my mind, despite the fact that it would be nice to see Mick do something on his own...

But not *permanently!* I always wished to see them back together again after a year or so of 'doing their own thing'. I did not want a permanent divorce between them.

Roxy Music had also split, or rather, Brian Ferry had such big personality clashes with Brian Eno that the latter had left the band. Another one bites the dust... Roxy Music without Eno really was not something any of us cared about so much.

The charts these days were absolutely *full* of 'Glam Rock', enough and more for everyone's tastes. I have suddenly put this in inverted commas...why?

Well. I had been there at the beginning, right at the beginning, with T.Rex. Seen them grow from baby glitterbugs singing about wizards, to fully fledged electrified satin-and-velvet warriors.

And then David! Try, just try, putting him in a box, really. Try to describe his style to someone in just a few words. Look how he changed drastically from album to album, from Space Oddity to MWSTW to Hunky Dory to Ziggy to Aladdin... It was a journey of a lifetime! And David would go on to change and change, again and again, much further, right as I had known he would even listening to his immensely diverse earlier songs.

As I said, this man will never bore me.

Roxy Music also had had their own style, for whilst Eno was swanning around in his random mix of feathers, satin and tat, Bryan Ferry and most of the others had worn suits, albeit trimmed with leopardskin collars, or topped off with purple platform shoes.

But now...

Okay, here we go. The newcomers were;

First of all The Sweet. These were four lads with long hair who dressed up in satin, silk, feather boas, silver platform boots, military uniforms and hot pants etc.

Some professional pop song writers wrote their songs in the main, Their music was basic, predictable, rhythmic, the words nonsensical but pretending to be interesting, with some silly voices and screamy bits in which one guy called Steve Priest pretended to be gay. None of the band was even mildly ambisextrous though. They lasted a few years in the same mode and probably ended up playing, in some format, at the end of British seaside resort piers in winter.

Now, Slade.

These were not a band formed on the back of Glam Rock; initially they were a kind of skinhead football-hooligan band who allied themselves to glam rock when it became popular.They wore all kinds of clothes in the beginning, and afterwards too, mostly tartans and 'tough' sort of pants and tops. But when T. Rex broke through with their Glam Rock look, which was entirely Marc's own wardrobe really, they began slapping on eyeshadow, tinsel around their hats, glitter boots and the like.

Although allied with and thought of as a glam rock band for some time because of this appearance, their songs were nothing to do with it and mostly were 'lads' and 'football' type chants co-written with a professional songwriter. They are probably still playing in Working Men's clubs and at Butlins in various guises.

There was a band called Mud, and one called Showaddywaddy, which both traded in on a kind of Fitiesised Glam Rock style for a while. Always these bands had four or five members of which one was supposed to be camp or gay. None of them was even mildly androgynous! The only Glam things about them at all were the costumes and this pretend 'gay' thing

Wizard were the only mildly interesting ones, led by a man called Roy Wood. This guy was musically gifted; he had a band called the Electric Light Orchestra as well, and mildly interesting to look at at least, with his 'big hair' and beard covered in silver, outrageous make-up and clothes.

You got the feeling with Roy Wood that he looked like that most of the time (sans make-up) as opposed to just for gigs, or on TOTP, and might actually be an interesting person. Their

music was quite clever, but did not inspire me.
And...beards...no. What are you hiding?

There were also two solo artists. One was alright, covered
Glam Rock as a style for some time in 1973 to 1975, singing a
different type of song before and after that period, and acting.
His name was Alvin Stardust after a few changes on the way.
His image was a kind of glammed-up, smouldering Elvis, hair in
a quiff. Really again just the costumes were Glam a bit, but
more leather, or better still, fake leather aka PVC. and he was
basically harmless and nothing to do with Glam Rock.

The other...well...

Gary Glitter is sadly as famous now for his recent activities as
he is for Glam Rock. His actual name is Paul Gadd, aka Paul
Raven, and although older and a carrying quite a bit more
meat than *my* heroes, he managed to convince older
housewives that he was as sexy as hell.

Which he was, in a way...but not quite in the way he projected!

He was not for me or my crowd; we original Glam Rockers took
none of these people seriously at all. But he did have some of
the best costumes, utilising mostly black and silver, and his
hair was in a Presley style quiff sometimes, but usually a huge
bouffant affair also sprayed with glitter or silver

His songs were apparently written by himself. They were not
overstretching on the lyric front; mostly repeated small
sentences or single words, like, 'Do you wanna touch?' "Yeah!',
lots of yelps and call-and-response stuff from his 'Glitter Band'.
He was quite obviously joking around and making a lot of
money from the Glam Rock scene without ever being any kind
of part of it other than the costumes, but he never made any
pretence of being an artist, only an entertainer.

Mostly we saw him as a harmless joke. Unfortunately...he wasn't harmless! Let's just leave it at that; those who don't know can nowadays use the internet to find out. This book is about Glam Rock and how it affected us then. So, then, he made us laugh a bit and take the piss, the kind of man my aunty Mary, who liked Tom Jones, might also like for a girls' night out.

So this is who we had now, no more heroes anymore, just these jokes in their various get-ups pretending to be like David and Marc, and this is why I felt lonely, alienated and depressed now. Not *really* so, as in big issues and shrinks and such, but a combination of teenage longing and almost-woman yearning.

And something else...

Even my friends were now not feeling the way I felt. For them, going to the concerts and meeting David had been the *culmination* of the summer experiences. For me, rather dangerously...it was just the beginning.

Of everything...

CHAPTER THIRTEEN – SOMEBODY TO LOVE!

Some time in July I had 'popped downstairs' to watch the Old Grey Whistle Test alone after pretending to go to bed; this way I was guaranteed a nice break from comments about tight pants and fairies by my dad, who unfortunately still had

Tuesdays as his Drinking Out With Uncle Don days and tended to become more testy and jeering in his comments depending on who was driving that evening.

But tonight I had got lucky; he had no night out with Don this week since the latter was presently on the family holidays, all was peaceful, not a creature was stirring, not even the budgie. So I made a slinky cup of black jo and settled comfortably in the armchair not more than three feet from the telly.

We never used to know who would be on. Not like nowadays, when everything is pre-known, preannounced and by the time you get it pre-watched more than likely. So it was rather a surprise when Whispering Bob Harris announced the guests for tonight and one group was called Queen.

Oh, really? Snigger, disparaging remark, mistrust of the name especially. But, well, we had faith in old Bob despite or maybe because of his whispers, so I settled down to watch what I hoped were not to be something else like Sweet or Mud. And this band began their first track of two, entitled Keep Yourself Alive.

Well, this band were certainly alive! And they could play, too. Despite not wishing to become a concert pianist or a music teacher as per my dad's wishes for me, my ten years of piano lessons had not gone entirely wasted; I knew a virtuoso when I heard one and these guys could definitely keep it together, especially the guitarist. I had never heard a guitar sound like this before; it sounded somehow like a whole orchestra at once.

The guitarist's name was Brian May. Fair enough. But it was the singer's name which had given our Bob some cause for sniggers and made me think they would be like some of the jump-on-the-bandwagon glitter rock bands who had followed in our Marc and David's footsteps in the wrong sized shoes.

One look at Freddie Mercury, though, was enough to tell me that whatever his name.....

Oh my God! This guy was sex on legs! Even at first glance I could tell he was not of English descent. Long, thick black hair whirled around his amazing face with its olive-toned skin. Superb cheekbones and a rawness which was ugly-beautiful depending on any given moment, and a pair of liquid brown eyes which you could drown in, rimmed thickly with kohl. A figure of more or less medium height, whip-slim, his chest bared to reveal something like a trophy rug glued to it, and.....more of those satin pants with bonus packs in them.

Freddie Mercury. This was him, then.

I was...

The middle part of OGWT crawled by in a blur of boredom. No videos and fast forwarding in these days; you had to remain glued to your seat in order not to miss a moment of the unrepeatable time of your hero on the screen. I made another very quick cup of coffee, peering urgently around the door as I waited for the kettle to boil. Then back to my armchair, craning forward as close to the TV as I could to catch the second track, Liar.

This song! I could not understand all of it but there was anger in there, and betrayal, and something about a priest. I wondered.....no, I knew, this song was a piece of Freddie Mercury's own life.

He tossed his head, arched his back into a bow, strode out, posed, postured.....truly a Queen. But in the regal sense, not that of a drag artist. Those kohl-rimmed eyes flashed sideways at the camera one last time, Whispering Bob whispered his surprise and approval, smirked a bit anyway again at the name.....and it was that man made of stars kicking a football and goodbye until next week.

I crept up to bed and lay there. I was hardly able to wait until the next day, when the Sounds music paper would come out and I could scour it looking for information. *Anything.* I had to see this band. I *had* to meet this man.

Slowly over the weeks I caught the trickles, the drops and even the perspiration of any new information about Queen. The summer holidays arrived; my family and I spent two weeks of them in Oban in the far west of Scotland, them dealing with the growing problems of the ageing Rockstarmobile, whilst I spent my time developing a fake southern accent, pretending to be an orphaned heiress, and picking up some random American boys to hang out with.

By the end of these, the music papers began to carry differing reviews, snippets and disparaging comments about Queen.

They had a new album out, that is the first thing I had found out. As soon as it was possible to buy it, I did, ordering it in at Wilson Peck since they would have been highly unlikely to stock it on spec.

I bought it...then I played it!

And played it...and played it.

I devoured the words of each song. No lyric sheets in these days, you had to listen very closely.

Nowadays I kind of had the Front Room as my room in the absence of a separate bedroom. I read and wrote in there as well as doing my piano practice, and I also used it as a design studio, spreading my fabric across the floor and cutting it and then machining it together, playing my records meanwhile.

The first track I ever heard of theirs was Keep Yourself Alive. Like I said, no lyric sheets, no ideas what to make of the songs except what came into your own head. This song sounded like it was about hustling, basically, trying to keep your head above water.

The sheer quality of the music was enough to blow you away after the sad dirges on TOTP lately. But added to all that, you had Freddie Mercury's superb singing voice and his authoritive delivery. Brian May's guitar is one of the mainstays of the group too, that sound! No-one ever made a guitar sound like he did, ever!

There was a track called Great King Rat. 'Great King Rat died today, born on the twenty first of May...'

My dad's birthday! Am I saying here...?

Troubles with my father were slowly escalating. The more I showed signs of wanting to be myself, whoever that was, the more he sneered at me, the more he put down.

But now I had this new confidence... "I think you're beautiful too, love..."

When the first person to tell you that you are beautiful, ever, is a gorgeous rock star...how can anyone else ever put you down again?!

But, he still tried.

One afternoon when I was about fifteen, a little group of my friends and I were sitting in the hall on a pile of cushions, at my house for once, chatting about 'what we wanted to do when we grew up.'

I was pretty clear on one point; "I want a room in London." We were quite organised for teenagers, and were speculating about how much it would cost, and how much you would need for food etc, and therefore how much you would need to earn, when my mum came back from shopping.

Well, no doubt she put the kettle on and made everyone a nice cup of tea/coffee but...when my dad came home, or rather, a bit after he came home, he suddenly had a rather nasty outburst about my desire to live in London!

I had absolutely no idea why he was so angry...but how had he known? My mother must have told him, eavesdropping on our conversation, acting all nice with the drinks, and then telling my dad whilst pretending to be friends with us.

But he was angry about what exactly? That I planned to leave my little town and seek work in the Big City?

And then he let rip one of the nastiest sentences ever thrown from father to daughter; "The only place you will ever get in London will be one with a red light over the door!"

So. Yes. Great King Rat. Freddie evidently had heard about my father already, and we had not even met!

Well, all the tracks on the album were interesting, esoteric in some way, hinting at subjects more than revealing them in their totality. But 'Liar', which opens the second side, is probably my favourite Queen track of all time even today. Like I said, I had glimpses into some personal anger of Freddie's. Had a priest...messed with him?

Freddie himself... Not many pictures were available at the moment as they were new, bubbling only in the music press and OGWT, plus SOTS of course but by now I *had* their album and as yet there were no other tracks to hear.

He fascinated me. He was truly exotic, I had never seen a man who looked like him. He had this thick mane of jet-black hair, dark eyes, dark body hair (!) and...here was *another* man with funny teeth. I must have a penchant for them!

Freddie Mercury had real buck teeth though, not just vampire fangs which he could hide. Every time he had opened his mouth on that brief show, these huge buck teeth would make their appearance. Large, unusual...and sexy as hell!

My fast-approaching womanhood energy was operating in overdrive mode now as I listened to his music or lay in bed at night...thinking...a combination of a naughty young Freddie in Public School, and what it would be like to kiss him, with those teeth...

Well. I would have to wait quite a while still to find out anything more. It was still only September...

I had already held my head up as schoolmates denounced Marc Bolan and David Bowie and now were being proved wrong. Here was a new cause to champion.

No-one had even heard of Queen at my school. The tour was finally announced. This year, though, when I asked Kim if she would like to come to see them with me, she was too busy studying for exams for 'the future'. Well, a) I was fortunate enough to be able to spew all that I had learned in a few hours' revision back onto an exam sheet as the same information in a different package without any trouble and b) if my future did not include meeting Freddie Mercury, and soon, I was not in it.

So I sent away for just one ticket. It was for the twenty-sixth November, and this time it was not nearby; the closest gig was at Manchester Opera House, where Queen would be supporting, of all bands, Mott the Hoople, whom I had liked for years, ironically more before their big hit with All the Young Dudes.

However...life was changing, speeding up pace. Things were coming gradually but inexorably to a head. I had, it seemed, only to focus on something with all my mind and heart and I could do it.

'Touching his arm'. Meeting David. Being...well...cuddled and almost swept up to his room by Mick.

And now there was this. Yes, in Manchester, not Sheffield, but I *would* go. Yes, it would be difficult and rather lonely, but I *could* do it.

And perhaps...I did not need anyone with me when I saw this band. Memories of 'can we have your autograph...?'

Because I wanted to really *meet* them. Really talk to them, have a conversation, not ask them for something. Them. Him. Freddie.

However, the last train I could feasibly catch out of Manchester was the nine thirty pm unless I was wanting to be on the milk train. So there would just be enough time to catch Queen, the support band, who would come on at seven thirty pm and be off by eight thirty latest. And there would just be time.....if I was lucky.....to pop around to the backstage door.....

I *had* to meet him, I had to. I had at least to try.

CHAPTER TEN – WAITING FOR THE MAN

I was now all a-quiver with anticipation about Queen's forthcoming gig, but this was still a couple of months away, and Mick Ronson's solo tour would not be until next year.

However...there was another impending tour about to hit Sunny Sheffield, and for this one I had a new partner in crime, my reunited old 'girlfriend', Simon Palfreman, since this forthcoming act was not a favourite with the others in my crowd.

But I had always found him fascinating, as had David Bowie himself, and already had one or two albums of his with his former band; now he was to visit Sheffield; the legendary Lou Reed, of the Velvet Underground, darling of Max's Kansas City, and self-styled King of New York!

Neither Simon nor I fancied Lou Reed, but to disciples of David Bowie this guy was the Legend, the ultimate in drawling chic, and we made sure this time to get front row tickets to see him.

Everyone David had ever spoken about in his interviews was investigated by his very-fast-growing band of hard-core worshipers, and it was thus that thousands of teenagers all over Britain became interested in Lou Reed and the Velvet Underground, Iggy Pop, Andy Warhol and his cast of strange characters, Jacques Brel, the French songwriter, Jean Genet, the French homoerotic writer, and other such random and fringe persona.

David and Mick (I felt confident now in referring to them casually by their first names since our 'encounter') had produced very strong, successful albums, Transformer for Lou Reed, now solo, and Raw Power for Iggy Pop, albums which I already had in my collection, along with a battered, wonderful second-hand copy of the legendary Velvet Underground Banana L.P. and a 'Best of Janis Joplin, an amazing American singer who had overdosed a few years ago, and whom some people said I looked spookily like.

Obviously now I had to complete the collection by going and seeing the two living acts as soon as possible.

Well, Iggy *did* apparently come to England for a brief spell, but went down like a lead balloon with his audience when he simply lay on the stage and stared at them instead of playing something wild, so he was not available. I was relieved in a way, as Mr Pop was most famous at that time for beating himself up with a dog chain, vomiting on his audience, cutting himself with broken glass, throwing the mic stand into the audience without heed to its destination, and pulling his pants down onstage to reveal his ass and apparently very large appendage!

I didn't mind that last bit, but the rest of it sounded like you might risk leaving the concert hall with anything from a dirty t-shirt to a broken nose, so it was over to Lou Reed, the more civilised of the pair by a long head.

His album, Transformer, was riding up the charts and with David taking a rest it was a good time for him to slot in the gap.

As I said earlier, this year Kim appeared to be taking more of an interest in her studies; 'O' levels were behind us and we were in the Lower Sixth, the first of the two sixth form groups. We were now Seniors, and some of my old friends had even elected to become Prefects!

I...truthfully no longer cared even in the slightest about school. My subjects were music, English Lit and Language, and French, but I had absolutely no idea of what I wanted to do with these. Unlike most of my friends, I was in an upper stream in the school but had virtually no interest in going to any college or University.

I was a rock and Glam Rock fan, an obsessive now about the amazing new music coming into my life, and the world outside of my twin interests of music and musicians, and designing new, crazy, outlandish outfits, was for me dull and uninspiring.

I was far from 'thick'. The school subjects simply did not interest me. I mean, yes, we choose the specialised subjects in Upper school. That does not mean, though, that you *like* them! It just means that you dislike the other subjects more... but school is compulsory, so you choose *something* because you have to. But the class reading is not necessarily what you would read if you had the choice...

One time, in Advanced French class, I 'awoke' out of the book I was reading avidly under the desk to find the teacher standing over me, repeating my name over and over to the astonishment of the class. She picked the book angrily out of my hands to berate me for reading rubbish...

...and discovered it was George Orwell's 1984. I was just at the bit when he was about to be tortured by the rats at the Ministry of Love...!

I received no punishment...

I just...did not want to be at school. But I did not want either to leave right now and be pushed to find a job in my locality.

I wanted...to be there. With my rock bands. On the road, doing *something!* Hearing their music every day, basking in their light.

I also had more than the average girl's interest in the gay world. Simon was 'out' now, and had met a slightly older boy called David during the summer holidays. Occasionally he brought him along to our house, where my mum, when introduced to 'Simon's boyfriend Dave,' never turned a hair and simply asked "Would you like a nice up of tea, love?" I don't think she was really aware of the connotations of 'boyfriend', and just thought it meant a good friend of Simon's.

Somehow I knew that my Glam Rock heroes all had some connections with the gay world. David Bowie was 'gay', he messed around with his guitarist who was not *technically* gay, but must be a *bit* gay not to mind...

Lou Reed was apparently bisexual, or transsexual, as were half the Andy Warhol characters sung about in Lou's songs or in Andy's entourage, including Wayne/Jayne County.

Marc Bolan was also apparently a bit gay, and there were rumours about Elton John. We didn't know about Brian Eno, but he was certainly camp!

So, it was with Simon that I made my way to Sheffield on a bright, sunny-but-chilly Saturday afternoon on the twenty-ninth of September, 1973.

Simon's hair was still in its Ziggy cut. I would retain my Marc Bolan hair for some years to come, made much easier by the discovery of The Perm!

There were in these days only two decent hotels in Sheffield; one was the Hallam Tower Hotel, scene of that glorious June afternoon's meetings.

The other one was much closer to town, the Grosvenor House Hotel. After my by now customary Posh Voice call to the first, I ascertained that Mr Reed and his entourage were to be staying at the latter...

We arrived at the appropriate time of around two thirty pm. It was only a short wait before Lou Reed and entourage arrived.

It was very quick, very decisive and very fast. There were about eight other fans there, and Simon and I, standing by the lift. The current version of Lou Reed, which sported very short bleached yellow-blonde hair, came in with a few people, looked us all quickly over, and asked rather brusquely "What do you want?" The other lot all asked for his autograph. Simon and I, in fact probably me, simply said "We wanted to meet you."

He thought about it for a millisecond, then inclined his head. "Come on then, you two!"

I have no idea why to this day. I think perhaps we were the only dressed up pair there, and evidently looked Warholesque enough to catch the King of New York's attention. I was wearing a dress which I had made which was definitely one of my favourites at that time. It was made of some kind of cotton mix, a change from my usual satins and silks, came down to the ground, or at least the tops of my seven inch platforms, was slinky and black with these strange little pink flowers on it, and a halter neck, which meant part of my back was bare.

But 'winter was coming' soon and already up north it was time to start donning layers. I therefore had ready a long black coat made from black panne velvet (very fine material, rolling up small enough to fit in my hippie bag) trimmed with white Maribou feathers, mainly for the pre and post concert chill.

My hair was really getting into its stride with this style nowadays and I looked almost exactly like the young groupie in Almost Famous, heels as high as ever, black mascara, nails and eyeliner and the obligatory glitter!

Simon was dressed up nicely too in what was basically a woman's fitted silky blouse and leather trousers. His hair blossomed a nice cherry red and he also wore eyeliner and eyeshadow.

So we got in the lift...with Lou Reed!

We really did have no idea where we were being taken. We were such devotees of whoever played the music we loved, and such Warhol Style Hounds, that we probably would not have complained too much had we been swept up into his room and asked to perform acts which Simon probably knew all about by now but I could only imagine, having gleaned rather a lot already from the pages of 'Querelle of Brest' and 'Our Lady of the Flowers'.

But in fact, the lift stopped at the third floor and we all got out and followed Lou into this kind of a coffee lounge and bar area. There were a couple of other people with him and he soon had it all organised, and Simon and I seated nicely by him to his right. Some other friend or two of his, also American, were on his left, but we were around a low casual table and therefore formed a sort of crescent moon shape.

He asked us if we wanted coffee, which I at least always did, and we said yes. And then he kind of...began to talk to us.

Not questions, not the usual sort anyway except to ascertain that we were coming to the gig. More...well, Lou Reed type of talk! New York jive, bitch slapping, Warholian in-crowd type of stuff, chatting randomly as though we already knew him, which perhaps in a way we did, through his music.

All kinds of subjects, lots about drugs. Almost like showing off, teaching the New Kids what-all they would need to know for the future. But he was not actually *doing* any drugs, not there and then anyway. Lou had in fact ordered a bottle of Bourbon alongside his own coffee, which he dutifully offered to us too.

Neither Simon nor I drank at that stage, we both had a whole night's concert to get through, a trip back on the bus and very strict parents, so we declined.

Lou kind of took the piss out of us a lot, mocked us. About not drinking, about not knowing about drugs, about not smoking even cigarettes (which he and his friends of course did), and about our accents. At one point I, ever the one to call a spade a mucky shovel, asked him "if you don't like us, why did you ask us up?"

He looked surprised then, all New York wide-eyed not-innocence. "I don't dislike you at all...just askin...'" he answered in that interesting drawl.

But I also was not really offended and neither was Simon. Somehow we knew it was all play to him, just something to do, something to say, some way to relate.

And...some pang of his own perhaps, trying to hark back to the days when *he* had not drank, smoked or done drugs.....was innocent...somewhere in his distant past, dimly remembered...

I kind of liked him. He was really sharp, witty, bitchy, funny. At one point he was telling us this story, involving his friend too in the details, about how they had once got an air bubble in the needle whilst doing heroin and had been convinced that they were going to die because they had read it was thus... It reminded me of one night when I was young; I accidentally stuck a lead pencil in my arm whilst watching TV with my great-grandma babysitting, and went to bed quietly, rather regretfully, sure I was going to die of lead poisoning!

Our accents fascinated him. He kept taking the piss and asking us to say things again and again, mocking, but again without rancour. I know he had already worked with Mick Ronson and they found it difficult to understand each other, but truthfully although he made a *show* of not understanding certain words and phrases at all and finding them ridiculous, in fact there was very little real difficulty in communication from either side.

The truth was...I think Lou wanted to know who exactly were his English fans. For sure he knew his own American crowd to a large extent, especially the New Yorkers.

But he knew full well that at least ninety per cent of his British fans came directly to him from David Bowie and his influences, and he wanted to know us, pick our brains, find out exactly what kind of people we were, what we knew, what we lacked, what we wanted...

Eventually it was five pm, he had to go up to his room and get ready for the gig. We said goodbye. I think he autographed something or other for us, mocking as usual; Simon had brought an album, but I just had a little notebook for autographs by now.

The autograph, as always, was the very least part of it for me. Simon and I went for a cheeseburger and chips before the gig, then we went inside and sat in our front row seats, went down to the front of the stage when the move happened, looked up at Lou Reed as he sang and played his songs of darkness and disgrace for us. Received a wink and a face-pulled grin at some point.

Lou Reed. We had spent the afternoon having coffee and talking about Heroin with Lou Reed. King of New York. David Bowie's friend. Rock 'n' Roll Animal.

Now I knew one thing for sure.

Anything was possible!

CHAPTER FOURTEEN – LIAR

The twenty sixth of November came slowly, slowly around. I am sure I did go to a couple more gigs before then, but as I said, Kim had become more serious about her studies and less interested in rock. She still, however, did have an enduring love for Free, Paul Rodgers in particular but the band in general.

They *had* in fact split up in 1971 about six months after we had seen them, to Kim's dismay, but then they had reformed again and released another album. But again they had semi-split and Andy Fraser had formed his own band, Sharks, who had opened for Roxy Music in spring.

Now, though, the members were all over the place; Paul Rodgers was in the process of getting his own band, called Bad Company, together, and Paul Kossoff was recording with drummer Simon Kirke and some American musicians. Kim was hoping that eventually one lot or other would tour and she would see her heroes once more.

Meanwhile, therefore, she was settling down to study; perhaps their split had lessened her interest in any other band. As for me...I was settling to...designing something new and amazing for the forthcoming Queen gig at Manchester Opera House.

Literally, *no-one* I knew had heard of them, and really their name was somehow not one to boast of all over the place in their as-yet unfamous state. So I kept quiet, appeared to be studying hard (re-reading Lord of the Rings and George Orwell's 1984 and such under the desk at school!). Meanwhile I worked out the train and other timings to a hair's breadth for the twenty sixth November 1973 with a fervour worthy of someone who might go on to hold a job at British Rail.

It all felt different on this night. I cannot remember where I had told my parents I was going. Not the truth. They rarely got the truth these days, since they had abused my telling of it. My mum was just a sidekick, but still could not be trusted as she, like many women of her age group, told her husband/my father *everything.*

I had turned seventeen on the eighth of November and so the questions were diminishing somewhat, as it was assumed that I was now studying hard for some kind of further education. No-one asked me, it was just...assumed, as it had been assumed that I would do well in my studies and pass exams.

My father had two ambitions for me. One was...a concert pianist. The other one was to be a music teacher, either in a school or privately. I was never asked. It was never considered that I might like to be a writer, or a designer. At present I was both...but neither.

I got off the bus in Sheffield and crossed the road to the train station. In these days you did not have to book tickets ahead.

There was a train around four thirty pm which would take two hours to reach Manchester. Although it was early, it was already dark as I reached the station; with the clock going back as per British winter time hours it would be dark as early as three forty-five pm in a month's time.

It was a kind of swirly, misty evening as I crossed that road to the train station for the ride which would change my life yet again.

Manchester is even more of a foggy, misty, drizzly sort of place than Sheffield, having as it does a set of shipping canals running right through its centre. I left the relative warmth of the train station and stepped out into the chilly, foggy night.

Manchester Opera House appeared, according to a street map I had looked at earlier, to be located quite close to some sort of canal area too. I had visions of walking along to be suddenly greeted by a deep, honking boom of a horn, and a huge ship passing close by, the hull sticking up eerily in the fog like the one in the Suez canal in Lawrence of Arabia...

But I did not come to any canal. Pulling my black Maribou trimmed velvet coat closer over my slashed old-gold velvet kaftan, which sat over my new slinky black satin, black sequin-trimmed halter dress, I ploughed determinedly along in the swirling mist on my seven inch platform heels, miraculously not breaking an ankle on Manchester's famously ill-maintained streets...

And suddenly I was there. Manchester Opera House, after all not right in the middle of the shipping canal, just simply there on a street corner.

I did all the usual things people do before a band come onstage. Get your ticket checked, go down the dark red carpeted aisle to seat whatever number it was (somewhere in the middle about twelve rows back, all I could get), check out seat placing as regards possible run to front, go off to toilet, have a piss, drink some water (wow, in those days you could actually take in your own water or drink from the taps!), drink a cheap paper cup of overpriced instant coffee, go for a piss, go check that no-one was in my seat, go to check make-up, go for a piss, take off upper coat and open slashed gold velvet kaftan (I had cut it down the middle, fitted it with hooks and eyes all the way down and added some trim), return to seat...

And then the lights went down, the band were onstage and Whammy! straight into their first song, Keep Yourself Alive.

Just like David Bowie and T.Rex, this band did not shuffle onto the stage finishing a fag and twiddling their guitar knobs. Just like the former two acts, Queen came on with a flash and with all the pomp and ceremony befitting their name, and befitting a headline act as opposed to a support band.

I *wished* that the crowd would stand up. Some people were actually quite impressed by Queen and certainly people were paying them more attention than many support bands got.

Me...

I had their first album and knew all of the songs, so I was already ahead of the game. Then Queen played Liar, my absolute favourite song of theirs, and I knew that I was going to meet them even if the train pulled out of Manchester without me...

Freddie! His lithe, catsuited grace, his dark, exotic looks, his long black hair, the way he tossed his head, turned regally and side-stared the audience.

Really, really a Queen. Never 'Queen' as in gay. *Always* Queen as in Royal. No matter what his future sexual proclivities, no matter the lavish use of make-up and hairspray and black and white satin by all the band...this group were the new Royalty of pop, rock, glam rock, whatever genre you wanted to name in fact.

I knew it in the first moment I saw them on the OGWT, and now I could see it for myself. Right now they were a support band only in terms of their position on the bill with a longer-serving act.

I scrambled out of my middle seat like a bat out of hell the moment the band left the stage, and straight out of the doors and around to the back of the hall.

"I want to see the band," I announced, big-eyed, to a kindly roadie somewhat taken by this pretty blonde weirdo hippie thing.

"You can't, love, they're just about to go onstage!"

"Not *that* band!" I exclaimed (as *if* I would be interested in the headlining act!!). "I mean the band who have just been on. Queen."

"Oh...*that* band?! 'Course you can go and see them, they're through there..."

The dressing room door was ajar...with a mini-knock and some trepidation but no delay, I walked in.

I stood in the doorway uncertainly, since it was like an outer dressing room and an inner one. There were a couple of guys in the outer one...none I recognised...I peered across the room...

...and he turned around, just in the doorway of the second room, and he looked into my eyes with those dark, expressive-beyond-dreams, bright, liquid brown ones. All I saw were his eyes, and I just walked into them!

I was standing, shy but indefatigueable, in front of Freddie Mercury. The lead singer of Queen. The man on the TV.

What did I open with? Something dorky...

"I've come all the way from Sheffield to meet you!"

Well, whooppee doo, and they had only travelled from London, wasn't *I* the little heroine!

But they did not treat me like that...

Some words from Freddie, some praise of me for coming. I told them I had seen them on the OGWT, which pleased them immensely. I told them that I had bought the album, which pleased them even more.

"How old are you?" asks Miss Dumb Q's of the year, gazing up into Those Eyes.

"How old do you think I am?" countered Freddie, flirting, buck teeth peeking out shyly.

"Er... somewhere between twenty and thirty," I stabbed vaguely.

"Oh, come, on, *that's* no guess!" laughed this beautiful, amazing exotic-beyond-my-dreams specimen, standing there by now in his lesser satin pants as opposed to his stage satin pants, a nice snuggly sort of fur-collar jacket-thingy up against his hair.

We established that he was twenty seven, had been so on the fifth of September (astrology being of huge importance to me; to him too had I known it...) and that I was just two weeks into my seventeenth year.

Virgo and Scorpio, then, we agreed, looking at each other.

He really liked my ensemble, the three layers of various long dresses, kaftans, coats. Currently I was wearing two and carrying the third; Freddie was really impressed with what I had done to the kaftan.

Suddenly from the other dressing room emerged a tawny lion, all blonde-and-brown tumbled hairsprayed locks and matching fur coat, big grin and huge blue eyes!

Roger Taylor, probably the best-looking drummer ever on the rock scene.

Some flirtatious, jokey exchange with us about what Freddie was talking about with me, then "Well, we've got to go. Are you coming back to the hotel for a drink with us?"

Can you believe me here? I mean, already with Mick Ronson, then Lou Reed...

"I can't, I have to get the train back to Sheffield."

"Oh, you don't *have* to, come on!" Freddie was looking at me.

"I do, my dad will kill me, he doesn't even know where I am..."

I think I got their autographs. I guess so, I needed some kind of proof, even for myself, some tangible evidence that what I have just told you was real.

And so it was goodbye for now, hope you are going to tour again soon, please play Sheffield...

Amazingly, the same kind roadie allowed me to sneak onto the side of the stage to catch ten minutes of Mott the Hoople's set.

I had always liked the latter band, for quite some years. Ironically the song which made me like them less was 'All the Young Dudes," David Bowie's gift to them, which had rescued them from doing a Free (splitting up) and catapaulted them up into the charts and now onto this tour. The song itself was good, and really brought out Ian Hunter's ability to lead a football crowd-style chant, but I hated seeing them all dressed up in the by-now-predictable 'Glam Rock gear, as they looked about as androgynous as a team of brickies and highly uncomfortable!

Still, I caught about two and a half songs before I had to leg it in order to catch the bloody ten past nine train back to Sheffield, giving me just five minutes to cross the road and catch the last bus too...

I sat on the almost empty train, staring at the seat ahead – I had a whole four seats to myself. I remember still the pattern on the seat covers, burning itself into my eyes. I simply could not get over this.

I had done it. I had met Queen. Freddie Mercury. All the band, in fact. Brian May was a very kind man, I knew that straight away, and I knew that I would never, ever consider him as an object of sexual adoration. And...shallow much...bass players never have hit the spot for me.

But Freddie, and also Roger as a fluffy Leonine back-up...

I guess I could just about make it through until their next tour...

More and more subterfuge and more and more lies lay ahead now. I myself was to become the Liar.

CHAPTER FIFTEEN – ALPHA BETA

Christmas 1973 came and went, and then it was 1974. There was very little happening in this time period; like the summer holiday period, I suspected that rock bands kept some personal time at Christmas and New Year, but that was perhaps because they knew their fans were also otherwise occupied.

I was not. School was just ticking by. I could not really see the point of it except in terms of keeping me from having to do something else, something which might be even harder to extricate myself from if an important concert came up.

Moneywise, I now used holiday times to work extra at Woolworths, so that was a bonus. I would need it. The coming year promised to have a lot of expenses!

First of all, on January twenty-fourth T. Rex played Sheffield City Hall again with their Truck Off tour.

In all truth...Marc and I had finished our romance now. I already knew it when I went along to see him. His music was great in the beginning when it was new, and perhaps if you were not a musician of sorts yourself you didn't mind that it had never progressed from the Electric Warrior album. In fact, there are so many people who find repeating a winning formula to be comforting and reliable.

But I – just like my David Bowie – have an unquenchable thirst for change, albeit it place, face, style or mind!

And lovely little Marc had, it appeared not the same attitude. He had found his winning formula with Get It On, Jeepster and Hot Love, then proceeded to write ten other songs with the same tunes, chord progressions and styles.

Now at Sheffield it was already a thinner crowd, and much easier to get to the front. Simon came with me this time, not Kim.

Marc pranced and pouted and swivelled his hips and rained glitter down on us just the same, tossed his curly head and smiled that irresistible smile.

But it was over. His time, at this time, was over. His ways, his songs, his look and style, were over for now.

For another man, his great rival since early days, had been behind Marc in coming to the top, but when he reached it, he had taken a look around, then put his arm out in a long sweep and scooped up all the eligible candidates for his own campaign, including the lost, the lonely, the sexually unsure, the confused, the rockers for whom rock was beginning to bore, the poppers for whom pop was beginning to be too twee and full of silliness, the searchers and seekers...and the T.Rex fans.

David had called us all, he the Pied Piper, beckoning us with his predatory, alien bedroom eyes to other worlds, sultry, sexy, camp, showy, outrageous, and above all *adult* worlds, and we had all gone with him. Even with David in America, our former idols could not win us back, for he had imprinted on us, and we were now his like sticks of rock, his name on our souls through and through from beginning to end.

Only the new and exciting could now entice...

In February Mick Ronson finally released his solo album, Slaughter on Tenth Avenue.

The cover was gorgeous, showing Mick in a stripey t-shirt and matelot's scarf, his blonde hair tousled deliberately, dark eyebrows arched, beautiful green eyes turned upwards, tears on his cheeks!

It was perfectly designed to woo a nation of girls and boys without their David for the time being. Our very own Rock God with a chance to prove himself as an independent hero. To play his guitar to death, to confound us with his own demonic visions, his own reality, his own fantasy worlds...

Of *course* I bought it when it came out. These things, music, concerts and fabric/trimmings, plus bits of 'antique' jewellery from Barnsley market, were my Must Haves.

My very first spin. My very, very first thoughts?

Oh, Mick, David had taught you to sing, or you learned from him, that is for sure. I mean, your phrasing, your delivery, the way your voice went up at the end, all were almost a carbon of David's style.

But not David's vocal power. You were always the perfect backing singer for David, Mick, always able to match your voice to his. But...lead singer is another story, for all the greats have their own style. You really *could* sing well Mick. But your style...your style was...David's.

What you excelled in, Mick, was the guitar! This is what we knew you for, this is what we loved most of all about you, even more than your gorgeous looks and sweet nature, was that long single note which formed the basis of the now-legendary Moonage Daydream solo. The desperate shrieks of Width of a Circle, the stallion screams of Time.

That guitar...

But although your guitar *was* present here and there on the songs, it was on only the Slaughter track and a bit of two others that it really came to the fore. Otherwise it was backing for your songs...

And the songs themselves...

The first thing I thought was, honestly Mick? Why on earth 'Love me Tender?' It is so not you!. *Singing* your heart out is not we need you to do; you can just play.

Play, don't worry.

But he obviously *had* worried about just playing,

Singing, much singing, much piano, much orchestration. Lots of drums and plenty of bass.

But it was as though his guitar was something he felt guilty about bringing out, like he'd bound it to David when the latter 'retired' and would only bring it out here and there in the future. As though he was apologising for being a guitar hero as opposed to a genuine all-rounder.

Most of the songs were only average truthfully. The first side certainly did not open any doors for me. The track by David was the only one which really moved. It was a little fast for Mick's singing, but it was a good song on which to demonstrate his David voice!

The other ones David wrote for him were the back-to-back Pleasure Man and Hey Ma Get Papa. Again, they were fast spoken-type singing rather than crooning, like David was trying to point him in the right direction.

And no-one can fault the wonderful guitar rendition of Slaughter on Tenth Avenue.

But very few of the songs are Mick's own work. There are many people today who slight David for not giving Mick writing credits on his albums, but to be fair, he is hardly claiming writing credits on his *own* album!

I played it a few times, but really, deep down, I was disappointed. I guess I wanted either another Bowie-style album, or something which really showed Mick's amazing guitar even if he did not sing much.

But this was a Tender-Sweet album sung by a beautiful man in a stripey t-shirt and a cute scarf and tasteful makeup, not the Gothicly dangerous rock hero who had ground down on a helpless David during a concert from outer space...

I am sure that David wanted the best for Mick. But you can put a seedling in perfect soil, water it regularly and give it the best fertiliser. However, the seedling can only grow into what it is supposed to be. You can't grow a rose from carrot seeds, and you cannot make a pack leader out of a subordinate.

Mick was being promoted, evidently, by his 'new manager' as a Romantic Hero. And apparently he was now also going out with Suzi Fussey, David's former hairdresser and wardrobe assistant.

We had met her briefly in Sheffield after David had gone up to his room. She was bringing in his luggage, I think, a kind of posh-voiced, friendly babe of about twenty-three with a brother who worked on the tour as well. He looked very like her, but it looked sexier on him. It was strange that she was with Mick now, since she had been all over it about David at the time! Still, I suppose now that he was away...

Despite what they played at onstage, David was always the Alpha, not the Beta. Mick was always the lieutenant, second-in-command. And it is sheer meanness to put up the natural second as a first; it is not his nature.

Well, here then was Mick's offering. Now we would wait for his tour and see if David would turn up on a white charger and rescue him.

I *had* read something a little strange somewhere around Christmas time; apparently David *was* supposed to turn up on his white charger, as a surprise, at Mick's debut pre-tour shows at Finsbury Park. But although he dismounted and parked said charger in one of the lanes ready to join his lieutenant onstage and fill him with the necessary confidence, somehow David Bowie was denied access to the stage!

It was probably at this point that he left for America!

So already I had seen T.Rex, and there was this from Mick, and it was only yet February.

However...

One evening towards the end of February, I was watching TOTP with the customary dim hope of relieving the usual boredom in these days of Ernie the Milkman, Two Little Boys and some inferior minor Glam Acts who had missed the first three boats. Well, the last act had been on before the countdown, and it was time for the song which played us out. I had almost risen and gone to make a coffee, when they announced....

'And now in at about number one hundred and forty two...The Seven Seas of Rhye by Queen'.

I was riveted in half sitting, half standing mode. I was almost sick with nerves as the song opened...this was *my* band, the band about whom I had said virtually *nothing* to anyone. My own discovery...and here they were, about to be judged by a nation!

You know what? I acted as though it were nothing this time! I didn't move, shush anyone or blink an eyelid as that incredible guitar sound flooded the speaker and Freddie appeared on the screen in his jet black satin catsuit trimmed here and there with just a little silver to break it up.

Whirling and prancing, flicking back his head in that defiant gesture, stabbing the mic in the general direction of the cameras, gazing into the main one...

I hardly dared to breathe as the song ended, anticipating scathing comments about fairies and tight pants again...

But since I had not reacted, not mentioned them in any way, my dad said nothing; in fact, he did not appear to have noticed!

Now I knew for sure how to play it!

March the eighth saw the release of Queen's second album, Queen Two. It was...quite amazing, one of the best musical ventures ever produced I think. There was a kind of concept about it too, one based in some ways on their style of dressing only in black and white.

There were two Queens on this album, the first side, The White Queen, written by Brian May, full of beauty and melody, the second side, The Black Queen, a dizzying collection of snippets from a fairy goblin's heaven and hell, written entirely by Freddie. He wrote like a painter!

However, the song I loved most on the album was The White Queen, by Brian May. They were a great partnership; Freddie's delivery of this beautiful song could never have been done justice by anyone else.

Freddie. I think I hardly ever called him Freddie Mercury either aloud or privately after that first meeting. He always was Freddie.

By now I had found out some facts about him...

He was of Persian origin, born in Zanzibar. His parents were civil servants, which is why he had come to England as a teenager. His hair was naturally jet black, then, his eyes that liquid brown. He really *was* exotic. He and Brian were classically trained in Music, and Freddie was qualified in Art too. All the band had music or art as their backgrounds and were very well educated.

I didn't need the Jackie magazines to tell me his age and birth date though. He had already told me.

There was one other thing I knew now.

They were touring again to promote this album. They would appear at Manchester University. On the twentieth of March.

CHAPTER SIXTEEN – THE WHITE QUEEN

The great advantage of telling your parents nothing about your new obsessions is that they do not suspect you of following them.

I knew that the Manchester gig would start late, it was a University. I knew that I would not be able to see much of it, if any. But now I was in the sixth form I had plenty of 'free periods' in which to 'study', and in which to take trains to Manchester early enough to catch the band in their soundcheck...

I knew also that I did not need to book any ticket.

It was a lovely evening. The day before the first day of spring, and doing itself justice. Gone was the swirling mist which had heralded my first connection with the band and in fact with Manchester. A late, low sunlight squinted through tree branches as England stirred in its winter sleep, woke up and rubbed its eyes.

I found the University easily enough, as you always do when you ask repeatedly. To this day I favour this method over Google Maps!.

It was about seven pm when I found the concert hall and stepped in.

The area was largish, spacious and slightly messy, a prefabricated feel to the place, like a temporary building of the kind you often found in schools in those days, as in mine. The door to the place was half-open and there were a few students wandering around.

I walked in and saw him straight away. The rest of the band were putting up their kit, plugging in instruments etc. Freddie, though, was sitting on a flight case, dressed right now as the White Queen, ie to the white end of the spectrum as opposed to the black, which would be reserved for the concert.

The minute I spotted him he became the only object in the hall, just as when I had met him last time. He was signing a couple of autographs. Already, then, there were other fans...

I stepped up onto the low stage where he sat. I simply...stood in front of him, watching him write something in the autograph books or on the albums of the other two. I didn't say anything, just stood there in my latest ensemble, Kim's borrowed droopy hippie bag over my shoulder.

As people often do in these situations, he felt eyes on him after a very short time and looked up.

There is no flattering and no denying here. He looked up into my eyes, and his glowed with recognition.

"Do you remember me?" I asked unnecessarily.

"Yes, I do," he replied, flicking his eyes at me and making a gesture for me to wait.

He finished off what he was doing and then must have kind of...dismissed them.

He patted the flight case for me to sit beside him.

The next hour and a bit went by in a whirl of chat, soundchecks and bustle as Queen were getting ready for their gig. It was a Uni gig so there was basically no division between the soundcheck and the actual concert; the hall began to fill slowly during the former, and the latter was not much more than an announcement away.

What did we talk about, Freddie Mercury and I?

We were both shy, I knew that, as I had known with David and Mick. In fact, do shy people make the best performers in the end?

Perhaps because we were *both* shy, we were less so with each other. One of the first things he spoke about was my bag, which was a Leo insignia when I had said I was a Scorpio. I told him I had borrowed it from my friend, so that was cleared up!

That led to chat about astrology and the crest of the band, which was made up of their four birthsigns and designed by them. Freddie, and indeed all the band, was into astrology in a big way, and any other kind of spiritual magic interested him too. Brian and Roger were also very much into 'being' their given astrological signs. I never did speak much with John Deacon; we would smile hello at one another but that was it. I never remember any other chat.

The next topic was...black and white nail varnish preferences!

Freddie was a Biba man, since he lived in London and had easy access to it, whereas I favoured Miners Black. We compared our fingernails (as you do with rising rock stars!) and I showed him what I meant; the black from Biba was rather flat and matte finish, whereas the Miners was cheaper but much more shiny.

Ah, the important things in life!

The others were tuning up and such by now.

Freddie had moved on to my jet choker by now. He had had a similar one before, he told me. "Is it real jet?" he asked. "Yes, I think so," I replied. "There's a way to test," he told me. "Give it to me for a minute..." I eyed him with surprise, then took it off slowly (I *never* took it off, but here was a man I loved even more than my jet necklace...)

I handed it over, watching to see if he was about to drop it in a vat of acid...

...and he bit it!

Freddie Mercury, of Queen, opened his mouth, produced those great sexy choppers, and bit lightly into my defenceless choker!

He had a good little chew, looked at it, then handed it back. I stared at him. "Real jet is soft. It's soft, so it's real," he added, pointing to it, having answered my wordless question of 'are you mad?'

Now I stared at it. For sure enough, in one of the beads were two tiny indents of Freddie's fearsome front teeth!

I put it back on slowly. He was teaching me things. This beautiful man, rock musician and rising star, wanted to *teach* me things!

It had a tiny bit of his saliva on it now, then. Another bit of DNA!

Shortly Roger came wandering over to see what we were up to, seated cosily side by side on the flight case, both looking weird as fuck I can now see in retrospect, all dressed up in negative and positive imagery (I was in black with my silver-blonde hair, he all in white with his jet black hair) inspecting each other's nails and chewing each other's jewellery...

A bit of a banter from his side and then he told Freddie the mics were ready to be checked and any vocal issues to be ironed out.

So then I got a how-are-you from him, a bit of a chat, and Brian May also came over to say hello.

He is a very nice man, Brian May. Above all, a humane human.

He had had some health problems recently, a bad stomach. And Hepatitis C. The latter was quite a hard-core thing to get and involved infected water amongst other things.

At that stage I think he thought it was something which would clear up, but it went on to take out a large chunk of his year.

Brian was a Cancerian, so he told me all that he knew about it, a quality of that sign, which has quite a liking for health issues and their details.

We also talked about the new album, which we were all excited about.

Well, now it was coming to that time before the guys would go onstage, as Brian told me towards the end of our conversation.

Freddie came back just then too. "We have to go and get ready for the show, so see you in a bit," he said.

Here we go... "I have to catch the train at ten past nine, though," I told him, "so I will only be able to stay for the first couple of songs."

"What, again?" "You see, I can't get a bus after eleven fifteen, and my parents don't even know I'm here..."

He gave me a mock-exasperated look, but one thing everyone has in common at some time in their lives is nagging parents, and so he did understand. I am sure he had done more than his share of telling fibs...

"Okay, then. When are you coming to see us again?"

Their tour did not pass anywhere near me after this gig, though. But they had plans to tour in the autumn...

"When you come to Sheffield or here or somewhere near next. Come to Sheffield, then I can stay and see you!"

The lead singer of Queen looked into my eyes then, lips slightly parted, buck teeth just a tease. "Okay, we will." "'Bye, then." I said. "Good luck with the tour." "Thank you." We held each other's eyes. People did not hug all the time then like they do now. His lips parted a little more in that famous buck-teeth shy smile, his eyes glowed, and they left for the dressing room.

I sat there for a while, went to the toilet, had a pee, drank some water, usual thing. The hall was really filling up now. I went right up to the front, against the stage...

And then some student head came on to announce them, the speakers made that sound as they jarred into life...

...and on came Freddie and the band, in a flash of light, launching straight into their first song, him whirling around like a dervish, posing and posturing, tossing his head, brandishing the mic in that way he had, his incredible voice soaring over the amazing music...

Now he was Freddie Mercury the showman. The shy guy who came alive onstage like someone had packed a rocket up him and lit it, as opposed to the serene, black panther-like creature who had sat chatting about birth signs and nail varnish.

He was quick-minded, highly curious and intelligent, truly 'mercurial' in his ways, but like an inquisitive squirrel whilst not onstage; it was there he became the third Lion in the band.

I had to drag myself away by the third song. I left quickly, glancing back over my shoulder and giving a little wave; they were well into it now and I have no idea if they saw me.

I knew that if I missed the train...I would wait and see all their set. And then I would be free afterwards, and so would they...

And secretly...I was not quite ready for this yet!

CHAPTER FIFTEEN – LOVE ME TENDER

In February, meanwhile, David had released a single from his forthcoming album. He was supposed to have a video for it on TOTP, but it did not reach the studio...that is why Queen had suddenly come on with Seven Seas of Rhye!

Ah, life! He moved over to give place for them then...and in quite a few areas!

It appeared that David was deeply into America at the moment. I supposed it niggled a bit, that he had given up his fans here for the American crowd.

With hindsight I realise he was very clever. He never allowed himself to go stale anywhere...something I have learned from him somehow, as I have learned so many other things from him.

And he knew one other thing about the British fans, us, the ones who had grown up with him from the vital ages of fourteen and fifteen when he had stolen into our lives. We, his 'children who came to boogie' would always love him.

We were already his, and even if he let us down and retired, changed his mind the following week, released a set of oldies instead of new stuff, and came back but to a different place as a different person, even if he did this a hundred times, we would *still* love him. Always and forever.

Now, these danged Americans...they were a different prospect! He had to stay over there for now, dig in his heels and really work on wooing them.

Apparently this is what he was going to do with his summer this coming year...

Well, I missed him. Missed his little carrot top bouncing around, missed his lean, athletic body with its milk white skin, missed his bare feet and long pale toes. Missed his odd eyes with that speculative look in them, like, 'hmm, perhaps we could...' Missed his strange clothes with the bumpy bits in them...

Missed him sooo much...

But now...there were at least other attractions.

First of all Queen...

And now, Mick was coming to us alone for the first time.

Mick was to play Sheffield City Hall on April twenty ninth, 1974. If you know anything else about Mick Ronson you will see the strange irony of this date...

These days I was going to concerts quite confidently alone if Simon was not able to come. I had found confidence in doing this from many sources; first of all, the success of my first 'Queen in Manchester' trip, the success of meeting artists which I achieved alone, and the fun of going sometimes with Simon, a gay man, instead of a group of girls (and the amusing fact that my dad thought it was 'safer' for me to go with a boy!).

There was also a growing group of fans of 'my sort of music' whom I had begun meeting at different concerts since the David Bowie one the previous spring. Now that my dad did not feel the need to pick me up afterwards, I could lurk around the backstage door a bit, and it was here that I begun to make friends with other 'regulars'.

There were a few girls, and one or two boys, whose names I cannot remember except for one girl, Michelle, who was quite small and thin and very pale and apparently had what was called an 'Overactive Thyroid'. It meant that whatever she ate, she stayed as skinny as a boy! The only downside was that she was very pale and had pop-eyes.

I began to wish that I had an overactive thyroid too, apart from that factor, for I had a naturally curvaceous figure and although slim, I had to watch every ounce. I rarely ate bread or potatoes, for instance, nowadays, or pastry, and certainly not biscuits or cakes. I had a fancy for yoghurt, fruit, lean meat, prawns, salads and, oddly, marzipan...

Coming from Yorkshire, this was not the most ideal diet to try to follow (except for the marzipan, which was sold by the block at the bakers next to the bus stop down in 'town') considering we invented Yorkshire pudding, and a good idea of a staple Yorkshire meal is fish and chips with bread and butter and mushy peas!

Well, now my Mick was coming to town I had to be whip-slim and carry absolutely no extra pounds, especially since the dress I was making had no space for such!

It was one of my killer designs; sheer as the north face of the Eiger and roughly the same colour, clinging to every curve, hump and bump, long but not trailing on the floor (you had to make allowances for that run to the front!) and basically body-hugging, except that I had made a little piece each side from the knee down which hung straight, but flicked out a bit when you moved; ie, a kind of kick-pleat.

This dress was to be worn only with...my latest seven inch black platforms!

I mean...literally.

In other words...no underwear. You could have seen the lines, you see, and I was just seventeen so there was no question of expensive invisible bras; although voluptuous, I did not really need one anyway. And the same went for pants.

It was a totally sheer dress, and saw me though about eight months of some of the most amazing concerts, times and adventures of anyone's life, as it turned out.

And it was made from...silver lurex.

Well, I guess my reputation was about to sweep back home in drag again...

These details nicely sorted, I began the organisation of the day well ahead.

Kim, Sue, Karen and Sharon, and also Simon, were all anxious to come to this one, and we had managed to get a nice front row line. It seemed only polite, too, to go and say hello to Mick...

However, we had school that day, so there would be no afternoon lurking at the Hallam Tower Hotel (yes, I had checked). So it would have to be *after* the gig as opposed to before...

There *was* a later bus than the direct one to my town, that aptly-numbered sixty-nine bus, which ran every hour up until about one thirty pm. That, though, went only as far as Rotherham and still left me with some five miles to go, so a taxi was probably necessary...

I had it in my head now that the ideal person to go Mick-hunting with was not any of my girlfriends, but my friend Simon. This was because...well, last time, for instance...

...and our successful meeting with Lou Reed...

And I suppose I was a little possessive of 'my Mick' too. Although it would be nice to feel that David and he had a little something going on at some point, I was pretty sure that Mick was not gay. For one thing, he had moved so fast that time with me that they must still be trying to get the scorch marks out of the Hallam Tower carpet!

So Simon was far and away the best choice. But how to persuade the others not to come...?

It was another fine evening, but chilly, as we walked up the long slope which led to the junction of the City Hall road, the Moor and the road to Cathedral Street.

Wilson Peck, the ticket and record store which had started it all, watched my progress with a raised eyebrow today as we passed by, noting how the little naive concertgoer had come along since its first gig just over three years ago in 1971.

I pulled my long velvet maribou-trimmed coat around me; it was actually too thin for the chill winds which could whip around Sheffield even in summer, but I was certainly not carrying my Afghan into gigs nowadays! Now it was only for use in winter as 'normal' wear.

I was fairly swanning around these days in my slinky dresses and high heels. I suppose I did look pretty good. The first time I had gone to a concert I was wearing a little bit the wrong clothes for the occasion and had no idea how to be Cool.

Now, I was the very epitome of cool, since my clothes went far beyond fashion. I was actually now...a designer!

Somewhere along the line I had taken a good look at what was available, compared to what I wanted the item to look like, and found the shops wanting. Plus, as a designer I could make the thing any way I wanted, fit it perfectly, add what-all trim and bits and pieces onto it, make the length right for me...

The four nights that I had attended the evening classes in sewing, which my dad had booked for me after the acquisition of the sewing machine, had taught me how to work with a pattern. I had then taught myself to *adapt* a pattern to whatever I wanted, using only the basics such as shoulder widths, waists etc, redesigning the rest myself. I could therefore make almost anything using the basic size/shape patterns I had and free-cutting the rest.

Simon's mum asked me to make something for his older sister somewhere around this time. She would pay me.

I made it, but it was to a set pattern and a standard size, therefore boring. I preferred to stick to making exciting things for me.

Back to the night.

There were quite a group of us tonight. Before we even reached the City Hall we had run into some people we knew from other concerts (the 'we' being Simon and I really).

Everyone was really excited. Yes, Mick was alone, but we felt he would bring some of David's sparkle and glitter along with him as well as his own beautiful self. So we were eager for the concert to start.

We girls eyed each other up now, wondering who would be Mick's kind of choice. Yes, it appeared that I was pretty, definitely the best-looking in my own little group, and Mick had responded to me for sure! But there were a couple of other contenders from the Sheffield gang who were also very attractive.

It was kind of nice, all the same, arriving at the City Hall and socialising with so many new people.

Something with growing up in quite a large family...you don't meet so many outside people. Others assume you have enough companions already and don't need extra people. And my parents, although welcoming to our friends, also appeared to think that our little group was enough for anyone.

But in a family, you have your 'place', your position, set down from childhood. It was Buddha who said that to become yourself you have to leave home. And although I had never heard of Buddha at this stage of life, I was already beginning to follow his path, breaking free of the mould in which I had provisionally been cast.

Even school has its rules and placings for children. A 'naughty' child in Junior school may still be regarded as such in his last year as a Senior, despite any changes to his behaviour. And your fellow pupils are likely in small towns to come just from down the road or at least only the next village, cast in the same mould as your own family.

But here in Sheffield were quite a diverse cross section of teenagers from a wider-ranging area, different classes and styles of upbringing. There were people, for instance, whose parents were 'not together', or who were the product of 'ships that pass in the night' and had no dad, so to speak. There were kids whose mums *worked* and they had to let themselves in and make their own tea!

My mind filled with personal alternative possibilities too...!

Let us just say that *these* kids were not always of a type whom my parents would have chosen as friends for me. Even as far back as their first meeting with Kim there had been a little rumbling in the jungle as to the fact that she lived in a certain area, and on a *housing* estate, no less! And when I had first begun going to concerts and my reports were less complimentary than they had been, my father even said it was Kim who was a 'bad influence'.

But now as the months, and years, wore on and Kim was studying every day, and I was...passing exams but beginning to spin out of his orbit...

...it was time for even him to admit that he was wrong. It was not Kim who was a bad influence.

It was his own daughter.

His own daughter even now was virtually leading her own little gang up the steps of the City Hall, following a quick, furtive check around the back door first just in case, by virtue of the fact that *Mick had put his arm around me and called me beautiful!*

We took our front row seats, put some of our stuff on them and promptly swanned off again, up and down the aisle, in and out of the foyer, showing off our outfits, chatting to some people I and Simon knew, nodding at others.

Strangely, I was never interested in drinking alcohol or smoking cigarettes. It never crossed my mind to do so! I think I saw it as a complete waste of money. No, those were not the transgressions I had in mind. Tonight...I was thinking for the first time properly of...

Well, I mean...so many invitations now to come to hotels, come inside, come...

And Mick so beautiful! Those limpid green eyes and huge long eyelashes, sexy contrasting black eyebrows, tanned skin, beautiful body, long silver hair...

And he was so friendly!

And he liked me...

And...and...

The support band played, as they do, to an audience which respected them for opening for the main act by their own invitation...but, hurry up, please, ah, is this the last song...oh, no, there is another one, a kind of 'ready' encore song for if the audience even clap slightly longer than expected...

Then they are off. And it's the interval...go for a piss, drink some water from the tap, adjust your dress (and in most people's case, your underwear...) go out, sit down in your seat again, wriggle around, head swivelling like a owl 180 degrees as you try to check out everyone you know even slightly to show off that you have front row seats, the coolest style and the best dress...shoot upwards four minutes before it's time, run off for a last piss, come back, get ready...

We only had to stand up and move to the front. Everyone did, cheering wildly. We took our place at the sacred Front of the Stage, from where we had watched Marc Bolan and T. Rex, David Bowie (and Mick), Lou Reed, Roxy Music...

And the lights dipped, and Mick Ronson took the stage for the first time in our town, alone.

He was *not* alone, of course, not really. He had with him his old mate and David's old bassist, Trevor Bolder, and the replacement for the fired Woody Woodmansey, Aynsley Dunbar.

There were rumours that David had fired Woody properly, not just 'goodbye, we love you!' because his ex-drummer was a Scientologist. We had know that all the time, along with each Spider's height, weight and hair colour, but it seemed now that it was no longer a good thing.

A lot of cults were coming up nowadays, that, and the Moonies, and others, and newspapers were full of reports from parents whose children were 'no longer their own', 'kidnappings' and strange practices. Now Scientology appeared to fall into these kinds of categories.

There was a piano player too, and perhaps someone else. But in addition to these...there were three female back-up singers!

Now, I am a rock-band girl. It might be Glam Rock sometimes, but it is still Rock, and not Doo-wop. And here were these three chicks...short slinky dresses and fishnet tights or stockings or something, all red and black, and they were definitely... Doo-wop!

Straight away, I thought, eh? Nose wrinkled, lip lifted on one side Scooby-Doo style. Like...what is *this* supposed to be?

In actual fact, all these people had hit the stage *before* Mick; as befitting his new star status, he came on after they had set the scene and prepared the way for him.

He was as dazzlingly beautiful as ever in his new outfit for the shows, pure white pants accentuating his lovely body and a stripey sort of matelot's t-shirt with a small scarf tied at the throat. A sort of sailor-cum-cowboy outfit.

The ladies, his back-up singers, were called the Thunderthighs evidently. Mick waved his seering guitar at us, tossed his long silver-blonde hair, smiled his amazing smile, and I sulkily half-forgave him for having these women in his show...

Mick had just one album out at this stage, so of course he played all the tracks from this. He also played a couple of the covers he and David used to play, like White Light, White Heat.

He played beautifully, and sang nicely. But...the one who sings harmony to the Main Man cannot always make the transition to singing solo. Mick has a 'nice' voice, a good voice. But it is not a strong voice. Not a lead vocal. Somehow he is still harmonising for someone who is no longer there...

I think we were all waiting for more Bowie stuff. Mick *did* play Moonage Daydream, amazing solo and all. But although the David Bowie music was present here...

...David himself was not. Not his voice. Not his lean body moving gracefully around the stage. Not his fiery hair, nor his outrageous costumes.

Not a feather falling off his boa. Not a long, pale foot extended in front of me. Not...an arm slung in casual affection around the shoulders of his guitarist, who I am sure would have appreciated this right now. Not a flash of his wonky canines as he grinned complicitly at us, his children.

And I was not the only one who noticed this. Not the only one at all. The whole audience could not help but notice the missing David by Mick's side, since the latter occupied only half the stage, not the whole, only the left side...

Subconsciously, throughout his whole set, Mick stood to the left and left a great, gaping hole to his right (I am speaking as I am facing him) as though by doing so for long enough would magically make a David appear in it.

And we could all see this, and therefore we too waited throughout the concert for the missing David.

If Mick had only just picked up his guitar and played it to death in his screaming Cyber-Gothic style costumes, black eye make-up menacing, boots glittering, and taken the whole stage as his own, band, Thunderthighs, the lot, he would have triumphed forever and the world might have turned a little differently.

But his songs...were more gentle, more melodic, more singing-based, less of the guitar for which he was famous. And the songs did not, as per the album, really fit him. There was nothing of Mick in them really, just some kind of an American Romance story running through them which had nothing to do with Mick Ronson from Hull, or the Spider from Mars who had clearly been David's personal favourite.

His outfits were sweet and pretty, his make-up subtle. He was playing a romantic singing hero, not the screaming rock god we had hoped to see. And he, always the Beta, so clearly missed his Alpha that you almost heard him howling in the moonlight along with his guitar.

We clapped, of course. We applauded, yelled, shouted 'Mick!' and sang along. We were his friends, his supporters, we were not going to let him down. We cheered him on and let him know he was great. We were there for him. We were his loyal fans...

But that is not how it is supposed to be, is it? We, the loyal fans, supporting the singer. Yes, of course it happens, a lot in the music world, the fans supporting their new artist. But it is not the mark of a Rock God Not the mark of one who can take you into the palm of his hand and mould you to his desires.

Like David. *His* David, who after all he needed, it was never clearer than when he was on stage now.

Like fluffy, tiny but so-confident Marc Bolan.

And like another, fast-rising star, my charismatic new friend Freddie Mercury.

These were true stars. True leaders, true solo performers for whom a band was necessary but for whom stardom on their own terms was guaranteed because of the enormous amount of confidence they projected.

The very confidence our lovely Mick lacked...

There should have been a Bowie-only encore, but instead some more covers. That story...that David had been there at the Rainbow shows around Christmas ready to step onstage during Mick's encore, and *the security had not allowed him!* By whose orders could this happen? Not Mick, for sure...

There was not after all an issue of ditching the friends before we went up to the hotel; everyone was now in the sixth form and studying hard; no question of them ligging about at hotels on a week night, if at all. Even Simon was not able to come with me.

With my photograhic memory, I had no trouble ingesting all the necessary information quickly in the morning and regurgitating it as something new in the afternoon; not so, it seemed, my colleagues. What price 'knowledge' and 'learning' if it comes so easily to someone...?

But the other friends, the new crowd, the ones my parents would not have approved of, these friends were more than eager to come up to meet Mick at the hotel, and so off we all trooped into the night, in our various post-Ziggy, pre-Goth costumes, up the long road to the Hallamshire suburb.

I was excited and somewhat nervous. Mick had definitely seen me during the show, noticed me, smiled more than once, winked. We were definitely 'on' in some capacity; what, I was not sure from my point of view, since I knew I could not get away with staying out more than a couple of hours longer tonight...

But still...I had to find out!

At first we lurked in the entrance to the hotel. There were at least seven of us and it was not guaranteed that we would be granted entry. But then Mick himself appeared, smiling at us all, many of whom he knew already and in his kind way he invited us all through to the bar area, where his little private party was about to increase in numbers.

There might have been other people there, other band members, just as when I met him last time. But really there was only Mick.

I sat and spoke with Mick as though I already knew him, as I did in some way. He too seemed to feel this. We were both shy, blonde, from Yorkshire and classically trained in music. There was some bond always in the Universe between Mick and I, which made two shy people not be as shy when together, and we sat and chatted for some while.

I cannot remember how the conversation progressed. I only know that quite soon into it I asked Mick about David Bowie, about their parting, which was never an official one, and whether they would work together again.

"I hope so," he said.

"Well, if you want to, why don't you?" I asked him.

"Ah don't know," he replied wistfully, gazing off into space. "He's in America now."

"Do you *like* touring on your own?" What a question, from a young fan to a star! But I have rarely been less than honest in life...

Again a pause, then a sigh. "Honestly, ah don't know," he replied again. His long eyelashes flickered thoughtfully. I was putting him on the spot...

And then he stood up and asked me to follow him into another, more quiet bar. His arms reached around my waist, around my silver lurex dress, and my arms naturally came up to link behind his neck. And he kissed me.

For the first time ever, unless you count an adventure with Barry Jackson and a girl called Wendy in the local quarry when I was eleven, I was being kissed by a man, properly, not a peck on the cheek, or even a chaste kiss on the lips, but a KISS.

And what a kiss this was! If any man ever knew how to kiss, Mick Ronson is that man. Bitch, please, I guess he had had plenty of practice! But WOW!

His tongue! I will never forget it, can still feel it. Like a feather, a butterfly, delicate as a cat's tongue, but sure of itself, as confident in my mouth as Mick was not onstage. Sweet and gentle but confidently exploring, flavoured lightly with the gin and tonic he had brought through with one hand whilst the other curved around my waist..

It went on for about five minutes, and when I stepped back for a breather I was conscious of being highly sexually aroused. I gazed up at him.

"No," was his response finally to my question of five minutes and a lifetime ago. "Ah don't really like being on me own."

"Then why...?"

"Well, ah've got a tour to do now, and another album to make...ah've signed a contract now..." he said gravely

I fell silent for a moment then. It didn't after all sound so easy being a rock star!

Then Mick Ronson looked down at me. "What shall I do, Di?" he asked me then. It was probably rhetorical, but he continued. "Run away wi' you?"

I gazed up into the lovely green eyes with their long lashes, the sharp nose, chiselled cheekbones. He was not smiling to take the edge off the words.

"But I'm only seventeen, and I live with my parents," I replied sadly. "And I've got to go home soon."

"Oh."

We both pondered this for some moments, then he leaned in and kissed me again for some time, after which we returned to the main bar.

Some Goodnights quite soon as the party slowly ended, and the whole little group of us trooped back down to the bus station to catch various night buses in different directions.

I and another two girls took the sixty-nine to Rotherham and then I alone spent some of my Saturday and other job money on a taxi home.

"What shall I do, Di? Run away wi'you…?"

Such a strange, poignant thing to say. And I believe he even half meant it. Even then, my seventeen-year-old self knew it was not the 'wi' you' bit which he meant most of all. It was the 'run away'.

I never did tell my friends that part. It was private, this was not Mick Ronson, Rock Star. This was Mick Ronson, extremely human being, baring his soul, to me, a seventeen year old fan turned friend. And…maybe lover.

CHAPTER SIXTEEN – KILLER QUEEN

Nothing had changed, yet everything had changed. Life appeared to go on as normal on the outside, but on the inside...how could it?! I had gone too deep now into the world of rock music and musicians, of rising and falling stars, to find interest, satisfaction and fulfillment in the everyday world.

School. What could anyone teach me of life now? I was learning things my teachers did not know. I was learning about music in ways which my father's private teachers had no knowledge of. I was getting to know musicians who did not read from sheet music, but from the insides of their own heads. I was learning about chord sequences, melodies and 'riffs' which did not come from an old tradition of music but were all new.

I was learning also about the reality of human life right now, here on this earth, in ways which no-one else could have taught me.

The truths of the music business were becoming clear. People did not just become rock stars and live happily ever after. They struggled to rise up and then, like David, found it all too much and took to drugs – it was becoming public slowly that he was using a lot of cocaine.

Or, like Mick, found alcohol and sex to be the appropriate props, lost as he was presently in his new and not-quite-suitable role as a Superstar as presented by his manager, the grasping Tony DeFries, the same who had wrung all but the very last drops out of David.

Like little Marc Bolan, who was now using both drugs and alcohol in excess and putting on weight, finding it hard to convince his old fans that everything was just fine and dandy in the garden and that the same old tunes revamped twenty times were just as good as some of the amazing new songs sung by other, more musically versatile singer songwriters.

Like Mott the Hoople, looking rather silly in their Glam Rock clothes when they were about as gay as a bunch of truck drivers.

Somehow now there was a kind of sadness, a poignancy in these conversations, too, these meetings. Now no longer the starstruck awe and blind faith of a thirteen, fourteen year old. Now no longer even the loaded yearnings of a fifteen/sixteen year old girl infatuated with supposedly unreachable rock stars.

Now the conversations were real, they were the private thoughts of rock musicians on the way up to stardom, or down from it, or on a plateau, shared with me, a seventeen year old schoolgirl who was soon to become a woman, showing me that these beautiful, talented twenty something men also had doubts, fears, also were unsure of how to play the game of Life.

And if *they* did not know...what hope, then, was there for the regular person on the street? If rock stardom was not the towering, glowing pinnacle of light it appeared to be, but only the tip of a volcano, with just as much chance to fall inside and be swallowed by molten lava like Gollum in Lord of the Rings...

But this all only made me more determined. I would not run from all this. I was somehow part of it all now. I could only be here. With it all. With them. We were all in it together now. Somehow...I could help...

I cannot remember much of the summer holidays. I think we had our family holiday in the Lake District this year. I got that nice little room (cupboard) under the stairs again. I took to climbing the mountains in flip-flops, hearing sneers of 'huh, she'll never make it!' from 'proper' hikers as I climbed up in denim shorts, vest top, sandals and enough jewellery to put a Pearly King to shame, and then exclamations of surprise as they arrived on top to find me already there...

I was spending less and less time around my family. My father was becoming more distant with me as I showed less and less signs of turning into a 'nice' potential concert pianist or music teacher, and more signs of becoming...well...a groupie! His comments were sometimes unwarrantedly sharp and sarcastic, 'mock-funny', for no reason other than that my life was not going his way.

I even spent less time with Kim, and more with Simon nowadays, and his boyfriend Dave, who he would bring around to our house quite a bit. The gay scene between men anyway intrigued me; something in me found it more 'normal' than the seemingly lemming-like desire of male-female couples to breed children. So I learned more and more about the gay culture, and the rock culture, and I felt more and more alienated from my family.

Everything was building, of course, to a head, a point, that tip of the volcano...

The last of my school years began in early September. But almost straight away also came the news that...Queen were to tour this autumn. And at last they would play Sheffield City Hall, on November fifth.

My home gig. On Bonfire night...

I got my tickets straight away, with no trouble, right at the front. Or rather, ticket, for I no longer checked if anyone else would like to come.

As it happened, they did! I can't remember whether it was through my constant talk about them since the previous November, and especially since their appearance on TOTP, brief though that had been, but in fact most of the usual concert friends had decided to come, around five or seven of the regular crowd, including Kim.

On the twenty first October Queen released their first 'real' single, Killer Queen. By real, I mean, full, planned appearance on TOTP, with Freddie in full flow, determined to dazzle, bewilder, bewitch and charm his way into the hearts and minds of all the young dudes who had recently been ditched by David, disappointed by Mick, let down by Roxy Music, and as for the remaining contenders...

And it worked. I think the moment he appeared on TOTP, their ticket sales rose and their fame became already guaranteed. But that was a bit later...

For now, they were just about to begin their tour...in dear old misty Manchester.

I had of course my front row ticket for the fifth of November. But...I could not wait. And after all, the tour kick-off gig on October thirtieth was not complete without their very first Superfan, the crazy one, the one so addicted that she would travel fifty miles each way just to watch them do a soundcheck!

It was indeed misty Manchester again that evening. This time I arrived really early, in time for the actual full sound check, around three thirty pm.

It was already becoming gloomy as per the British manner of clocks going back in winter, and true to form the Manchester fog began to swirl around the backstage door of this time the Manchester Palace Theatre. Some roadies arrived before the band themselves, and as roadies are apt to do when faced with an attractive blonde seventeen year old, they let me in out of the cold.

Queen came along soon enough. I was already seated comfortably a few rows back from the stage, a lone audience for the rising stars, who greeted me with happy exclamations and how-are-yous, Freddie talking as usual about jewellery and clothes, and Brian explaining the details of his latest health crises, which had caught up with him big-time in the summer; he was only now recovering from it all.

And we were *all* talking about their new music! After all, it was almost my project too, my pride and joy, we had already come some way together and we all knew it.

It was really cool watching them do a full soundcheck with their new material. I realise now that I heard it before anyone else except their recording people, families and friends. I loved the tracks, the new style was harder-edged than before, and there was a certain raucous challenge from Freddie in some of the vocals which had not been so obvious on Queen Two, like this album was carrying straight on from Queen One.

Soundchecks are quite long affairs, or were then anyway, about one and a half to two hours. A roadie offered me a cup of coffee in a plastic cup; I discovered where they were making it, in a makeshift 'kitchen' area at the back of the hall, and offered to do the next batch, which I did, handing them to my heroes onstage and the road crew alike.

Around six thirty pm was the train which would take me back to Sheffield in time for me to appear just to have popped there for shopping after school, something I was wont to do sometimes nowadays, so I said goodbye to 'my' band, whose leader gave me the usual rolled-up eyes as he discovered that I was not even to stay for a part of the concert tonight.

This time...a kiss on the cheek. I told him I was trying to arrange to come to Leeds too on November the second, still a few days before the Sheffield gig...

Long, deep looks.

Liquid brown eyes in mine.

I was drowning in love now, and I knew that something very big was going to happen very soon.

It just had to be Perfect. I had to set the stage, I was setting the stage...

Train.

Bus.

Back to my parents, having been 'at Kim's', when she had not even been interested that I was going in the first place! Nowadays my school mates treated a concert for what it was to them, an interlude in life. Not life itself!

The second of November found me again at the stage door mid-afternoon, this time in Sunny Leeds. The weather was definitely getting colder and I had dragged the recalcitrant Afghan coat along on its lead for this gig.

This time as soon as the band arrived and we had said our Hellos, I was into the makeshift kitchen area and making us all coffee. I already knew how the band took theirs!

I watched them doing the soundcheck again. Already the reviews were beginning to come in, and apart from a couple of bitchy ones who would continue to criticise Queen throughout their career, most of them were very positive, especially about the music. As with David and Marc, there would always be critics who did not approve of their style of dress and camping it up onstage, but again, as with the former two, this was to prove an asset ultimately and not to their detriment.

After this soundcheck I had an hour or so before the blessed train would take me back to Sheffield. Freddie called me up to sit with him. Probably on a flight case again; in those days they lay around at the edges of the stage, waiting to be repacked again after each concert.

We talked about this and that, as you do. About music, and jewellery, and clothes, and more importantly, about their performances and music now.

I was sitting there with him, with Freddie Mercury, a shy Persian-Indian mix man of twenty eight now, long, glossy jet-black hair a little dry and with split ends, as he pointed out, from so much straightening, beautiful, hopeful eyes shining now as the culmination of his life's efforts approached.

He turned to me then, flicking those shy eyes up at me in true Indian style, had I known it. "Why don't you come on the tour instead of coming and going all the time?"

Dead silence filled the space for some seconds. Why don't I...what?

My mouth must have dropped open.

A couple of shallow breaths, a missed heartbeat...

"I can't..."

I think I had got him to sign something else of mine, for no reason, just because... since he was holding a pen. He flicked my long, curling blonde hair with it then.

"Don't be silly, of course you can!" he replied, smiling shyly, flirting.

Oh...

I cannot remember exactly what I replied, since my insides had turned to liquid...this was after all what I had dreamed of...but how would I explain...?

"Well, I can't now. Today. I have to go."

A questioning look...

"I...have to go home today..."

"Alright..."

"Sheffield. I'll be at Sheffield. I'll come...in the afternoon..."

My voice tailed off...

He looked at me.

"I'll...see you, then...?"

"Okay. 'Bye for now..."

My heart was thumping, my head in a whirl, all the way back on the train. I had *said* no. I had still deferred the decision until later. I had still put him off again...!

How I wished I had been able to say yes! But with my strict, unpredictable father on my tail now at every end and turn, I had no idea what would happen if I just...

...came to the show...?

CHAPTER SEVENTEEN – NOW I'M HERE

And here I was. At the backstage door at the City Hall, Sheffield. I was there only twenty minutes or so when a couple of the roadies arrived with the equipment and let me in. They all knew me now, since I had made coffee for them...

There was excitement in the air now, a kind of tension. The band were a week into their tour, and the reviews were coming in thick and fast. Queen were literally on the pinnacle of their success, just a wobble here or there, to one side or another, and they could still fall.

There was even a little tension in this soundcheck, Freddie and Roger having a little screaming tiff at each other about some technical point at some point. These next few weeks were for them the most important ones in their career as it turns out, just as the ones for David had been during and around the Starman on TOTP showing, and for Marc around the time of Hot Love.

The difference here was that there were four equals in this band. Freddie was the frontman and the showman, but there was never any question of him lording it over the others. Brian May held the whole project in the palm of his calm hand ultimately, as there was no guitar in the world which made the sounds he could produce from his. And Roger was certainly not 'the drummer' in this band, he was Roger Taylor, The Drummer with Queen, and the girls sought him out almost equally with Freddie.

So. On through the soundcheck we went, and then it was over.

"Are you coming to the hotel with us?" asked Freddie.

I was almost sick with nerves, and with the fact that I never used to eat anything all day in order to fit into my skinny dresses, but I nodded. "Yes, I can come. I'm coming to the gig too..."

It was the Hallam Tower Hotel again, already the scene of other meetings. We took the lift upstairs.

Freddie was in room 405. I went in with him nervously, walked to the window.

"Do you want some coffee?"

Well, of course I did; he ordered it on the phone.

It came with some side biscuits, which I picked at under Freddie's direction, although my stomach was already full of butterflies.

And then we...sat and talked!

About him, about me. About my schooling and what I wanted to do versus what was planned for me. About the fact that Freddie lived with a lady called Mary, whom he loved very much, there was never any doubt about that, but who did not come on the tours generally; she had her own life separately from his.

I was...the Music Girlfriend, I suppose, the one who followed every note, every change in pitch, every difference in his voice on every song.

For I was to be that. This is what he was offering. If she would come to any gig I would have to stay in the background. They were not married, but he called her 'my wife' in his quiet, cultured voice, his teeth always getting in the way of words to create a special accent.

But...I also had a place. For whatever reason, neither of us could fathom. But...Freddie Mercury, who I had adored and wanted from the moment I saw him on the TV screen and for every moment since, who I had travelled to meet just for an hour, four times now, wanted me in his life. At least at this point in time, we had some kind of destiny together.

Was it enough for me? This role, in this tour?

Would *you* have said no?

We drank coffee, therefore, and ate biscuits, and talked now about design, fashion, music, clothes, jewellery, nail varnish, art, fantasy worlds and astrology again, as we had before, all the time, now that the basics had been shyly settled between us. That would all come together...tonight, after the show. For now...

"Are you hungry? We are going to have some food before the show..."

I had brought a little bag with me, with a few spare clothes, some perfume and a toothbrush in it. I left it there...

Queen, as I discovered along the way, usually ate together, band, road crew and all; breakfast was a big gathering, and evening meals before the gigs same. So now I sat down to steak and vegetables with the band and some of their road crew.

Their promoter at this time was Mel Bush, an big-overcoat-wearing kind of guy, and their manager was called Norman Sheffield (ironically!) I never spoke with Norman at all, although Mel Bush was friendly enough. Mel would sometimes be there at the dinners, but Norman did not appear very often.

Well, soon enough it was seven pm, and we all piled into the cars for the short trip to the City Hall. I got out with the band and was around with them for some minutes, and then I left them to changing into their satin and tat and took a trip into the auditorium itself, since my friends had come...

I suppose I *did* want to see their faces when I came not from the back of the hall but from the side of the stage and dropped down to chat with them. I arranged that 'since I would be backstage' someone of the group from further back could have my front row ticket, since I no longer needed it...

I honestly do not know what they thought. Although I am sure they were green with envy, I guess they also thought that I had totally gone over the edge now. I was definitely no longer one of them, and I knew it as I said casually, "Well, enjoy the show! I have to go back now..."

Which I did if I wanted to be in my allotted space at the side of the stage in time for the performance...! Just as casually, I mounted the stage and returned to my new place, amongst a new set of friends.

And for the first time ever, I was able to watch my band, Queen, play an entire set as a headline band.

It was with an extra edge now that I watched Freddie. My eyes were riveted to him, you could not have peeled them off, he, with his long black hair tossing about, his back arching, the pelvic thrusts, the way the white, then the black satin (there was a costume change mid-set during Roger's drum solo) stretched tight over his...bonus pack...

The way he held the microphone, now roaring into it, now crooning seductively...

The band were so tight, so brilliant. There might be a moment of screechy-whiney feedback from Brian's guitar here, a dropped stick from Roger there. But these are the wonderful perks of seeing a band live as opposed to hearing a record.

The audience had mostly only heard Killer Queen and perhaps a few more tracks. Most people had come to this gig on the building rumours about this new band. They had not known of them more than a year ago, bought their first or even second albums in the main until recently, if at all. But Queen were the New Big Buzz, and to miss them was to be left behind, so the hall was full, and by the end of the gig the fans were yelling and pushing at the front of the stage.

The set was a full promotion of the new album, with an equal mix of the first two albums thrown in. There were also a couple of covers thrown in for novelty value, like 'Big Spender' and Jailhouse Rock'.

One of my favourites, though, was a new song called 'Lap of the Gods', which came in two parts really, 'Lap of the Gods Revisited' being the second part. They played both parts, the second one near the end. It was an amazing song, written of course by Freddie, dramatic and strangely emotional and spiritual. It was somehow my 'song of the tour'...forever.

The dry ice pumped out, the lights flashed, the 'thunder' of the drums roared...

Freddie and the band did their final encore, there was another flash of 'lightning' and then the band disappeared.

Coming to as though from a dream or trance, I followed back to the dressing room...

My future was now.

In the Lap of the Gods.

I never could settle after that Queen tour of autumn 1974. Went back to school, did not tell anyone the details but everyone knew, since it was pretty obvious, what I had been doing in the three weeks I had been 'absent'. My eyes must have been different. My manner certainly was, and as for my accent I now spoke with a semi-London one, my speech littered with 'dears' and 'darlings', my eyes flashing at people to make an impact and probably my nose in the air for the most part!

Ultimately my temper lashed on some woman with her kid who treated me like a second-class servant when I was serving her in Woolworths one Saturday, and I was fired.

My father had stopped my pocket money entirely as a punishment for being a naughty little groupie, bringing shame on the household (!) by not coming home one night in November, and for many days more except for some clothes and to collect any birthday money owed and do my Saturday job...after which it had been off on the tour again to Lancaster, Preston and Bristol. And then again down to London for the final two shows...

I had kissed Freddie goodbye quietly and privately at the end of the tour, for Mary was around at these two London gigs and I had agreed just to be there and keep quiet.

I knew things were changing for the band; interviews had increased during the tour, and a Moet et Chandon representative arrived one day to present the band with a 'Methusalah,' a special gigantic bottle of champagne for their mention of the famous French company in 'Killer Queen'.

There had been increasing tensions with the band and their current manager, and Freddie, who lived on a knife edge emotionally anyway, was very upset by some of the stipulations and restrictions he laid down on the band.

When we said goodbye there was no mention from either side as to what would happen next. I lived in Yorkshire – at least at the moment – and he lived in London, with Mary and some cats.

I was going to do...I was not sure what. And he...was about to become very famous, and was both welcoming and dreading it.

So...it really was all in the Lap of the Gods.

I had done something which had barely seemed possible a year and a half before when I had first seen this band on TOGWT, curled close to the TV in a chair drinking black coffee and yearning for some kind of an exciting life. Now...I had been on tour with them. With Queen.

I heard many years later that Freddie was gay even back then. Well the truth was...I never saw him with any boys. Or for that matter, whilst I was on the tour, any other girls, except for when Mary was around.

Freddie *was* certainly one of life's great experiencers, ready not only to taste but to gobble up what the future had in store for him. The following year they would go on to be managed by John Reid, who also managed Elton John, and it was then, since I did go to some of those gigs too, that I saw a change at least in his public manner.

For now, I awaited the next episode of what the Fates had written for me.

CHAPTER EIGHTEEN – WAS A WIZARD

It was autumn 1975. I had lived in London for some months. I had stayed first with a roadie friend, then in a hostel; now I had a small bedsit with sink and cooking ring. It did not have a red light over the door.

I had this daytime job in a betting shop in Central London, and the evening job in Fulham at the well-known rock venue The Golden Lion.

I had been signed up for three evenings per week but ended up working almost every night since I never got tired of the banter, the vibe of rock, rock, rock twenty four seven three six five.

Of famous rock musicians dropping in for a pint whilst we pretended not to recognise them, and the rock bands themselves who played every night from nine thirty pm to eleven pm. In these days there was an eleven pm closure on all British pubs, ten thirty pm on Sundays.

However most nights saw us either drinking late in a pub lock-in, usually with some of said rock musicians, or at a party to which one or another of the bar staff had been invited by a couple of girls or boys who would look horrified when at least ten of us from the pub would troupe in.

I used to spend my time in between jobs or on days off at a place around the corner to which someone had taken me one afternoon. The name of this place was Manticore. It had been an old cinema, but now belonged to Messrs Keith Emerson, Greg Lake and Carl Palmer, who used it as a recording studio and rehearsal auditorium and hired it out most days for the same purpose to other bands, hence the plethora of such in our pub.

The Golden Lion had therefore become well known as a cool sort of place, where rock stars could drink in peace whilst random customers of the pub who were not 'in the know' would remark sotto voce to their friends 'don't that bloke look like Robert Plant!' and then agree that it couldn't possibly be him...

Well. Back to Manticore. I had been introduced at some point to Keith and Carl; I did not really know Greg. The former two were genial and easy-going and I took to using their little office as my regular drop-off hangout between this and that.

There was a guy called Colin who usually answered the phone and such, but quite often he was absent, so I used to do it myself, and since there was a book for writing down whoever had called about studio and rehearsal time and the like, I began to help out in this department to the extent that it became a sort of third job. Plus I made a nice cup of coffee or tea with enough regularity to satisfy the most ardent addict, could sew well enough to repair torn pants and shirts and was a useful little creature in general.

One day I had the daytime off, only working that night, so I popped into Manticore around lunchtime. I had pressed the buzzer and been admitted, and as usual had asked who was 'in' today. The reply was rather scathing. "T.Rex," Colin informed me.

"Oh....."

Memories of being thirteen and entranced at this very pretty creature flashed into my mind. I was now a knowledgeable, definitely not virgin nineteen year old who knew for sure what lurked beneath tight satin pants; I felt almost a pang for my youthful crush.

"Don't you like them?" I asked Colin. A stream of invective poured from the mouth of this rather supercilious young man about the musicianship of the now out-of-favour T.Rex, ending with "I can't stand *him* either. He's coming in soon and I really don't want to have to talk to him, he's so full of himself. I need to go out to Hammersmith as well.....but someone has to make him coffee and look after him, he's paying enough....."

Thought bubbles must have erupted above my head in clusters at this point.

"Well, *I* could make him coffee and look after him and show him the place....." "Oh, could you? I'd be really grateful..."

Strange. Once long ago I did a kind of quiz-cum-seance in Jackie magazine. One of the questions was "Will I ever meet my hero?" The answer was quite ahead for such a magazine; "You will, but he will no longer be your hero."

So a little time went by and then the door buzzer rang, Colin answered it and after some moments he came up to the office, followed by.....

There had been stories that Marc Bolan was now an overweight washed-up talentless joke, but the truth was that his fairy castles and wizards were no longer the vogue; sci-fi and cynicism had replaced myth and magic for this time in the world, satin and velvet were being replaced by synthetics. He had simply fallen out of fashion.

But to my astonishment, the petite creature who followed Colin into the office was the exact same beautiful young man I had fallen in love with six years ago.

He had hardly aged at all. His perfect, elfin features were still enchanting, and his corkscrew curls had grown from a mistake of a cut back into the halo I had so envied in the past and still managed to emulate, these days with the use of perm kits.

He wore some strange, colourful patchwork jacket with a collar of fake leopardskin, as it was late November, which made him look even more attractive and cute, and velvet pants and Cuban heels; we had all stepped down somewhat from our platforms these days...

And so Colin introduced us, me as 'anything you need, ask Diana,' and went off to Hammersmith leaving us in the office together.

I was always making something, some top or skirt or dress. I no longer had a sewing machine since it was somewhere in my dad's front room in Yorkshire, so I stitched by hand; the results were nonetheless unusual, since I still refused to be led around by the fashion nose. I made Marc and myself a coffee and sat back down with my sewing. He took a seat quite easily on the telephone table and began to chat.

Marc Bolan doesn't ask, so what's your name and where are you from, what do you do, etc. "Have you read Tolkein?" is his kind of opener, and it was here that we connected immediately, we gelled and I knew that my teenage instincts had been right; this young man is not from this dimension really. He never was. He was not in it for very much longer as it turned out.....

Well of course, Marc Bolan was not here to chat to me about Lord of the Rings or Narnia. He had rehearsals to attend the next day and it turned out he was just checking the studio out today and sorting out details. He went out to do all these things and popped back from time to time. In total in the space of about two and a half hours we had around an hour of chats and coffees.

The touch of his presence was as light as a feather, his easy smile as ready as a child's. I have since read so much about how egoistic Marc was, and how vain and monopolising of attention. I found none of these things about him. What I did find was that he was truly and deeply into the magical world, it was not just an image, he really believed in it all, wizards and warlocks and goblins and spirits.

He sat cross-legged on the table most of the time as he had sat onstage the first time I saw him.

Yes, his conversation was littered with 'man' and 'cats' and 'love and peace', but that was the way of the times just preceding these more jaded ones.

He disappeared again for a while and when he returned I was packing up my sewing as it was time to go to the pub and work. We hugged goodbye, he a little taller than me since I was in my virtually flat bar shoes, not heels, and he was wearing small heels himself. His fluffy curls brushed my cheeks and he smiled that sparkly smile which seemed to come complete with invisible glitter.

That night at the pub I mentioned that I had met him. Immediately there came a round of groans and hoots and derision, words like 'pooftah' and so on. I just shrugged and carried on, not bothering to argue.

I knew who I had met. I knew something of the real person now, because to be truthful, Marc Bolan, the rock star and Marc Bolan, the elf man in human form were one and the same. There was absolutely no division.

He was complete and whole. There was no bullshit, no outer image to be defended. Marc was simply Marc. His confidence might have been a little shaken by a troubled previous year, but he was back on form now and the sweetness inside and the sweetness outside merged into one, and that one believed wholeheartedly in himself, myth, magic and music.

For the first time since I had begun working at the pub, I knew that these people were wrong, they were fallible, they didn't know everything. And I knew too that today I had been really lucky in meeting and connecting with a great soul.

Less than two years down the line, Marc would be dead in a car crash, just as he had always feared, his girlfriend, not himself, the driver, but still, his end had come as he had more or less predicted it.

I have visited that place, now a shrine to Marc kept by an ever-adoring fan. The willow tree which claimed his life is serene and hung with garlands and little notes. I wrapped one of my long, now black, dreadlocks around a small branch as a token to Marc for inspiring my life-long fascination with strange, mystical hairdos.

The place is surprisingly peaceful, and Marc's life-force, his laughter and glitter smiles are now in the trees and bushes around.

Paul Kossoff from Free went to sleep on an aeroplane during a flight to or from a tour gig and never woke up; he had overdosed finally on the heroin which had dogged his last few years and had a heart attack during his sleep on the flight. He was just twenty six.

Freddie passed over in 1991, dying of AIDS-related pneumonia complications at the age of forty-five, a world superstar. I went to a tribute concert for him in which thirty-two people tried to sing songs which one man had managed alone, and failed. No-one ever had that voice.

Mick Ronson followed in 1993, dying of liver cancer. He too was not long meant for this world, my sweet Mick, who pined away for his Alpha in some way.

Trevor Bolder, the bass player of the Spiders from Mars, also died of cancer, aged sixty two, in May of 2013.

Lou Reed, undisputed King of New York, died in 2014 without giving up his crown at the age of seventy-one in October of the same year.

Keith Emerson died in 2016, closely followed by Greg Lake. I visited Manticore recently. There is now a Waitrose on that hallowed spot, and the Golden Lion has become a sad flat-screen TV 'trendy haunt' which no-one visits. Yet, if you look up, the Golden Lion is still there on top, surveying Fulham proudly from its roof.

Most of all...greatest of all...hardest of all...my David Bowie passed into another dimension last January. It is listed that he died of liver cancer after an eighteen-month battle and was burned in a Buddhist ceremony with no friends or family present. He had just completed the mysterious Blackstar album and an amazing if puzzling musical called Lazarus.

Who knows, with David? His ever-changing personas all life...is this just another of them? Elvis is English and climbs the hills...

And me? As usual, roaming around, selling my handmade wares, writing, reading tarot, chatting about more interesting times, travelling Asia, never content to settle. How can I, when, like my heroes, I will never stop seeking that indefinable something which I do not even know the name of?

Now, with the passing of so many Seventies heroes in these last few years, there is ironically something of a revival. Glitter sparkles on everything, and I just saw a pair of silver six-inch platform shoes in a shop in Brighton for a hundred and thirty five pounds!

Ah, if only I did not have a father who threw out everything not nailed down if it was more than six months old...

My autograph books, other little signed items, photos, clothes, Afghan coat...all have gone. My father never did really forgive me for 'going my own way' as he put it.

But I have such memories etched into my soul. Such faces, eyes, bodies...such music...and most of all, such inspiration!

And they are all with me inside my heart, ready to greet me again one day in some form or other; who knows what it is which lies behind the door?

Angel or Devil, I don't care,

For in front of that door...there is You.

What would have happened in my life if David had not gone to live in America for two years after the autumn of 1973? Would it all have been different then, if he had toured, if we had met again, if it had been *him* the first time? Or if it had been Mick (who again came into the picture a little later along the way)?

I ask him. David...Would it have been any different if...?

And he opens a window in the fabric of time. And shows me.
No. It would have been no different, whatever the way. You are
as you are, and this was all always meant to be.

So now I can move on, with him, as always, guiding me.

Diana Wilde,

23rd August 2017

THE GLAM ROCK FILES

Printed by Amazon Italia Logistica S.r.l.
Torrazza Piemonte (TO), Italy